THE CHRONICLES OF OJII-CHAN

Jon Shirota

TotalRecall Publications, Inc.
1103 Middlecreek
Friendswood, Texas 77546
281-992-3131 281-482-5390 Fax
www.totalrecallpress.com

All rights reserved. Except as permitted under the United States Copyright Act of 1976, No part of this publication may be reproduced, stored in a retrieval system, or transmitted in any form or by any means electronic or mechanical or by photocopying, recording, or otherwise without prior permission of the publisher. Exclusive worldwide content publication / distribution by TotalRecall Publications, Inc.

Copyright © 2016 by: Jon Shirota
All rights reserved

ISBN: 978-1-59095-461-4
UPC: 6-43977-44610-7

Library of Congress Control Number: 2016939096

Printed in the United States of America with simultaneous printing in Australia, Canada, and United Kingdom.

FIRST EDITION
1   2   3   4   5   6   7   8   9   10

The scanning, uploading and distribution of this book via the Internet or via any other means without the permission of the publisher is illegal and punishable by law. Please purchase only authorized electronic editions, and do not participate in or encourage electronic piracy of copyrighted materials. Your support of the author's rights is appreciated.

For Barbara

Author Bio

Jon Hiroshi Shirota was born on Maui, Hawaii. After serving two years in the U.S. Army, he graduated from Brigham Young University and became an Internal Revenue Agent. He quit his job when he was invited to the Handy Writers Colony in Marshall, Illinois (From Here To Eternity fame) where he finished his first novel Lucky Come Hawaii.

Jon is the recipient of several awards: The John F. Kennedy Center Award; The Rockefeller Center Award; The American College Theater Festival for New Plays; The Best Stage Scenes of 1992 by Smith and Kraus Books; and a grant by the Japan/USA Friendship Commission and the National Endowment for the Arts to spend six months in Okinawa doing research of its immigrants to the United States.

About The Book

Ernie Pyle, America's greatest war correspondent, covered the battle fronts in Africa, Italy, France and Germany. Then, during his last assignment, he was killed on tiny Ie Jima off the coast of Okinawa.

There have been speculations who shot Ernie Pyle. Grandpa Ojii-chan who was in the battle of Ie Jima fighting for Japan alarmingly discovers that he could have been the one who had killed the famous non-combatant war correspondent.

Table of Contents

Chapter 1: Flight from Honolulu	1
Chapter 2: The Long Journey	10
Chapter 3: Naha	21
Chapter 4: Ie Jima	30
Chapter 5: Ryudai	50
Chapter 6: The Translation	60
Chapter 7: The Invasion	68
Chapter 8: Mabuni	80
Chapter 9: Kudaku Island	87
Chapter 10: Pig Feet Soup	100
Chapter 11: Ishikawa POW Camp	109
Chapter 12: Yogi Park	118
Chapter 13: Rumor	127
Chapter 14: The Photos	139
Chapter 15: Turmoil	151
Chapter 16: Solitude	164
Chapter 17: Rainstorm	176
Chapter 18: Partial Moonlight	194
Chapter 19: The Spot	207
Chapter 20: The Pronouncement	213
Chapter 21: Revelations	217
Chapter 22: Missing Chapter	222
Chapter 23: To Last Shot	226
Chapter 24: The Ring	228
Chapter 25: Speeches	235
Chapter 26: The Engagement	237
Chapter 27: Sayonara	240

"Jon Shirota, a skilled and compassionate writer, has recreated the spirit of iconic journalist, Ernie Pyle, in *Chronicles of Ojii-Chan*. Shirota has recaptured Pyle's long career as an evocative writer and will engage new sets of readers."
--George Henrick, writer, author, critique and professor of English literature, Emeritus, University of Illinois.

"Jon Shirota's novels have always been compelling readings. This story of Ernie Pyle's death on Tiny Ie Jima island has more than a ring of truth to it."
--Ray Elliott, is a marine veteran, and former president of James Jones Literary Society and author of *Iwo Blasted Again* and *With The Silent Knowledge*.

"From my office window in Nago, I can see Tiny Ie Jima where most of Jon Shirota's story, *Chronicles of Ojii-Chan* about the death of Ernie Pyle takes place. It is an intriguing and suspenseful account of how America's leading WWII correspondent had died."
--Katsunori Yamazato, writer, professor of American literature and president of Meio university.

"Jon Shirota's *Chronicles of Ojii-Chan* is a skillfully plotted novel, his best to date, telling a compelling story that also pays tribute to Ernie Pyle."
--Ed Sakamoto, journalist, playwright, recipient of three pookeia awards, Hawaii's most prestigious awards for excellence in writing.

"It was a pleasure and an honor to translate portions of Jon Shirota's warm and suspenseful novel *Chronicles of Ojii-Chan*.
--Marie Yamazato, adjunct professor of English, university of the Ryukyus, and a former aide of Masahide Ota, the venerable governor of Okinawa.

Chapter 1:
Flight from Honolulu

He looked out the window. It was a typical spring morning, the mountains draped with light misty clouds, Diamond Head a clear gray-green, the roof tops of the Aiea homes and Tripler General Hospital sparkling under the morning sun.

He was sitting in economy class next to the window. Passengers, mostly Japanese nationals, were rushing in, scrambling to place their carry-ons in the overhead compartments. They all had leis around their necks, some paper, some flowers, some with freshly woven lauhala hats on their heads.

He pinched off a petal from his lei, brought it up to his nose and inhaled deeply. Ah, the sweet fragrance of ginger flower. It was from the same plant he had planted not long ago. And Carrie, their daughter, had made a hurried lei and placed it around his neck as they got into the car. Then it was Carrie, not her mother, who drove him to the airport. Her mother, as expected, was too busy to come to the airport and see him off.

The seat beside his was still empty. He looked up front at the line of passengers coming in. Who is it going to be? The old lady with armloads of gifts? The old man searching for his seat? Or the big fat haole white man in an oversized aloha shirt. So far nobody. Maybe, the seat will remain empty. And he could have both seats all the way to Tokyo.

A young girl about Carrie's age approached the seat. She had a carnation lei and a pikake strand around her neck.

She looked at him; then again.

"Professor Yamashiro!" the girl said. Jubilantly.

Oh, Christ, he thought. Must be one of his former students. Now, she'll be talking all the way to Tokyo. He did not, however, recognize her.

The young attractive college girl placed her carryon under the seat before her.

"Are you going to Japan on a vacation?" the girl asked.

He shook his head. "Were you in one of my classes?"

"I wanted to, last semester. It was filled."

"The American Lit class?"

The girl nodded. "I should have known better than to wait until the last minute."

"You're local?"

The girl shook her head. "From Okinawa. An exchange student."

That explains her proper English, he told himself. No Hawaiian pidgin accent. She must have spoken English since childhood. Maybe grew up in the States.

The girl stretched her seat belt, leaned back, adjusted her belt and leis.

"Are you lecturing at a university in Tokyo?"

"In Okinawa."

The girl was overwhelmed again. "At Ryudai."

He looked at her.

"Ryukyu Daigaku."

He nodded. "University of the Ryukyus."

"An American Lit class?"

"Contemporary American Lit class."

"I'll have to sign up before it, too, gets filled."

"A graduate student?"

The girl shook her head. "A senior. I have another semester to go."

"Do you know Professor Miyazato?"

"Professor Miyazato? It was he who suggested that I apply for the exchange student program at University of Hawaii."

"Liked it at UH?"

"Yes. I loved it."

"It was Professor Miyazato's idea that I apply for a fellowship at Ryukyu Daigaku."

"You are friends?"

He nodded. "Graduate students at UH way back. Before he went on to UC Davis for his Ph.D; and I went on to UCLA."

"I heard about you long before school started," the girl said.

"Me?"

"Everyone in the English department talked about you."

"Oh?"

"Especially when you chose books about Hawaii for your classes. "From Here To Eternity." "Lucky Come Hawaii." Michener's "Hawaii…"

"Ever read any of them?"

Yes. I loved them. Especially "Lucky Come Hawaii" about a Hawaii Uchinanchu family."

"You're Uchinanchu?"

"A true Okinawan. Both sides of my family Yamashiro," she went on. "You could be Uchinanchu or a Yamatunchu from Mainland Japan."

"Uchinanchu," he said. "On both sides."

"Nisei?"

"Sansei. My grandparents came to Hawaii to work in the cane fields in the early 1900s."

"Where in Okinawa were they from?"

"Motobu."

"Motobu! We're practically neighbors."

"Oh?"

"My grandparents' home is in Ie Jima."

"Iwo Jima?"

"Ie Jima. It's just a few minutes boat ride from Motobu. You've never heard of Ie Jima?"

He shook his head.

The flight attendant came on the speaker. She announced, in her Japanese accent, that all handbags be placed under the seats or placed in the overhead compartments.

This was his first trip on a Japanese airline. It would take approximately seven hours to Tokyo. All his other trips had been eastbound to California on United or Hawaiian.

"Oh, I'm sorry," the girl now said. "My name is Reiko. Reiko Kinjo."

"And I'm Chris," he said.

The girl, Reiko, smiled a warm smile and nodded respectfully.

He nodded back.

The airplane, its jets not quite roaring yet, began rolling backward. The flight attendants, all Japanese, walked up and down the aisle, making sure everyone had his/her seat belt secured.

Chris could now see Hickam Field and Pearl Harbor to the left, the morning traffic on the freeways to and from downtown Honolulu congested as usual. Well, he thought, no more fighting the traffic to UH Manoa. At least not for a year. He had heard that the traffic in Tokyo is worse than in Honolulu. In Okinawa, too? he wondered.

"Where in Okinawa are you staying?" Reiko asked, leaning over slightly, gazing out the window.

"Naha."

"Are you commuting all the way to Ryudai?"

"Is it far?"

"Well…"

"Takashi… Professor Miyazato found an apartment near the monorail. He said it was convenient."

"It is going to depend where you'll be staying."

"Either take the monorail or a bus to the campus," he said.

"Which monorail station?

"Asato Station."

"That's near Kokusai Dori, the main street in Naha," she said. "He must've found you an apartment at Kina Mansion."

"Kina Mansion?"

"That's what we call the condos in Okinawa. 'Mansions.'"

Mansions? He hoped they won't cost as much as the mansions in Honolulu.

The jet engines were now roaring, ready for takeoff.

The girl, Reiko, leaned back against her seat, her eyes shut. When the plane finally went airborne, she looked over at him, somewhat relieved. "I'll never get used to the plane roaring off and climbing so fast," she said.

"You're okay now?" he asked.

Reiko nodded and inhaled deeply, a warm smile returning to her face.

Not encouraging the girl to keep up a conversation, he reached down into his handbag under the seat before him and brought out a book he had started reading a couple of days ago. "To Reach Eternity." It was about James Jones, author of "From Here To Eternity." He had discovered the book while browsing through a used book store in Kaimuki. He was surprised that he had not come across the book much earlier. Since he had lectured on Jones's "From Here To Eternity," he wanted to know everything there is to know about Jones. The book was written by Professor George Hendrick of University of Illinois. The campus at UI was in the same area where Jones was born and wrote his classics after his discharge from the Army. Who knows? Professor Hendrick might have known Jones personally. According to the book jacket, there are hundreds of letters that Jones had written over the years. From his combat days in the Pacific through a colorful and impressive writing career. Maybe, he'd use the book for his lectures at Ryudai. "From Here To Eternity" would be a good book for the Okinawan students who knew quite a bit about Hawaii where the story takes place. Adding Jones' letters would make it even more interesting.

While partly immersed in the book, he thought of Hawaii when he was still a young student at UH. So much to look forward to; the whole world your field of dreams; no makau as the old Hawaiians used to say. Nothing to be afraid of.

And today... Yeah. And today. Taking a sabbatical leave. Getting away from things he once cherished: a good marriage, a wonderful daughter, a tenured professorship at UH. Jesus! How things can change. Without warning. Well, a suspected warning.

Damn that bitch!

And, she had even tried to deny it.

Even when confronted with indisputable evidence.

Jesus!

In a way, it was a good thing this fellowship came along. They both needed time to think things over. Not their marriage. That was all pau. Finished. Down the drain.

It was now how to settle their assets. The house, their stock investments, their IRAs. But not the farm in Kailua. She thought it should be a part of the settlement. Hell, no! That farm was an inheritance from his dad. All his. After buying out his brother Roy's share.

Damn bitch! Threatening to sue for her right to that property. Her right? She had absolutely no interest in it. Not a penny!

The girl, Reiko, apparently bored and wanting to continue their conversation, turned to him.

"Is it interesting?"

"Huh? Oh, yeah. About a favorite author of mine."

"James Jones?" she said, looking at the book cover.

"Heard about him?"

"I read several of his books. "Eternity," "Some Came Running," "The Pistol." My favorite, of course, is "Eternity."

"Mine, too," he said.

He turned the page of "To Reach Eternity," hoping to discourage the girl from continuing their conversation.

He, of course, could not tell Carrie the details of her father's and mother's pending divorce. Why make it worse for her? Poor kid. Caught in the middle. He didn't know what her mother had said to her, but he was sure she blamed it all on him. Probably even told her he was involved with some woman.

When she herself was cheating on him!

Jesus! How a wife can twist things around! And really believe it, too. Oh, sure, he was tempted to fool around with a student or two. Especially when the kids came throwing themselves at him. But that's as far as it went. He never touched any of them. And damnit! They were pretty, too. And sexy. Oh, boy, were they!

The temptation of a college professor, he mourned silently. Always there. In your face. Sometimes, begging him to… He managed to fight it off though. Had to. Get involved once, there's no end to it.

Look what happened to Greg Singleton? Poor guy. The

temptation was too great. Couldn't let it pass. And the young girl wouldn't let him forget it. Got called into the President's office. Resign gracefully or get kicked out disgracefully.

Anyway, he managed to fight off the temptations. Oh, don't get him wrong. He's just a man. The temptation was always there. With the same urge as any other man. But...

And so that's where they are now. Rose and him.

They'll let their attorney, their same attorney friend, tie up the loose ends of their divorce. They'll split everything. Except, of course, the Kailua property. .

The girl, Reiko, indicated the book in his hand.

"You're having difficulty concentrating?" she said.

"Huh? Oh, this book. Must be the plane ride. Going away from home, and all that."

"Do you have any children?"

"One. A daughter. Got through UH. Now a graduate student there."

"Her mother, she's a college professor, too?"

"Nah. A business major. Now, a vice president at Royal Pacific Bank."

"A vice president?"

He nodded.

Yeah. A vice president. Got there sleeping with the president, he wanted to say.

"You must be proud of her. And your daughter, too."

He nodded. Carrie, yes. Rose? She can go to hell.

Chapter 2: The Long Journey

He's never heard of Ie Jima, she told herself, her ears adjusting to the altitude and the roar of the jet. For most outsiders Okinawa was the only island in the Ryukyu archipelago. When actually there are countless islands in the chain of islands from Japan to Taiwan, some inhabited, some uninhabited.

The professor, most likely, has never heard of Ernie Pyle either, she thought. Why would he? Ernie Pyle was in the Second World War, a war in the distant past. She, of course, knows of Ernie Pyle, a little at least, because of the Ernie Pyle Memorial Park on Ie Jima.

And also because Ojii-chan Grandpa was the caretaker of the park. Ever since she can remember Ojii-chan used to take her to the Memorial Park and have her help water the plants and rake the leaves. Not to mention polishing the Ernie Pyle plaque.

She did not know why Ojii-chan had dedicated his life to the park, nor if Ojii-chan really knew anything about the American, except the American was a war correspondent who landed on Ie Jima with the invading forces.

What little she knew about Ernie Pyle was that Ojii-chan thought highly of the man. Why? She did not know. After going to the park all those years, she began feeling that she had known the man and the man had been a family friend. Especially on April 18 of each year when she joined Ojii-chan burning osenko incense, placing them at the plaque and bowing very solemnly to the words before them.

The professor held his book before him but obviously not reading it. He seemed lost in another world. An absent-minded professor? she thought, laughing to herself. He doesn't seem old enough to be the father of a graduate student. Most likely married while still going to school. He can't be much older than forty. Quite good-looking, too. With a warm friendly smile.

She hesitated, then finally asked, "Have you ever heard of Ernie Pyle?"

He looked at her. "Ernie Pyle?"

"You've never heard of him?"

He held his head inquiringly.

"He was buried in Ie Jima."

"Ernie Pyle... Ernie Pyle..." his head still sideways. Finally, "Oh, Ernie Pyle! The war correspondent in the Second World War."

"He was buried in Ie Jima."

"Not the same Ernie Pyle we're talking about," said the Professor. "He's buried at the National Memorial Cemetery of the Pacific at Punchbowl. In Honolulu."

"Before that he was buried in Ie Jima," she said.

"You're sure?"

"There's a memorial park named after him."

"On that island, Ie Jima?

She nodded.

"I know he was killed in Okinawa..."

"In Ie Jima," she corrected.

"Well, somewhere in Okinawa anyway."

"Not in Okinawa," she corrected again. "In Ie Jima."

He looked at her.

"Okinawa is Okinawa. Ie Jima is Ie Jima."

He finally gave in. "Yeah. Right."

"If you want," she added, "I'll be glad to take you to Ie Jima, and show you the memorial park."

"Well…"

"I don't mean right away. Someday, when you're settled, and have some time."

"Sounds good."

"It's a beautiful island just a few minutes ferry ride across the bay from Motobu," she went on. "It's famous for Gusuku Yama, the only mountain on the island. A lonely pinnacle really, reaching 600 feet straight up into the skies. The island is also known for its warm, friendly people. For its famous play also."

"Play?"

"It's put on every year, and people from all over Okinawa come to see it."

"Must be a great play."

"It's a tragedy. Like one of Shakespeare's."

"Oh?"

"It's about a love affair between a fisherman shipwrecked on an isolated island and a woman who rescues him. The man goes back to Ie Jima. The woman waits for his return. When he doesn't, she goes to Ie Jima looking for him. She discovers that the man is already married and has several children. Devastated, she climbs up Gusuku Yama and plunges to her death."

"End of play?"

She shook her head. "When the man discovers the woman's body, he is grief stricken with guilt."

"He commits suicide?"

She shakes her head.

"He lives on?"

She shakes her head again.

"Gonna keep me guessing, huh?"

"The man goes mad. He kills his wife and children. Then, climbs up the mountain and jumps down to his own death."

"Wow!"

"Okinawans, like the Japanese from the Mainland, love romantic tragedies."

"What's this one called?"

"I'll Meet You At Gusuku Yama."

"I'd like to see it someday," he said, non-committingly.

"I'll be glad to take you," she said.

The professor nodded, then went back to his book.

She thought she'd better leave him alone. She was being overly friendly and taking too much of his time.

Poor man, she thought. He's already missing his family.

What kind of a woman is his wife? Obviously very intelligent to be the vice president of a bank in Honolulu. And most likely very attractive the best hairdresser, the most elegant cosmetologist, the richest Dior dress shops. Undoubtedly, a socialite in the Honolulu business circle. Must be very exciting married to someone like her.

She felt a grin creeping up her face.

She almost had an exciting relationship in Honolulu. Well, sort of. If you can call it that.

She had really believed that Jimmy Crandal loved her. That he would marry her.

Oh, how foolish she had been!

An innocent Okinawan girl lost in the fast lane. The dazzling auto lights blinding her.

Almost comical now. Yet still painful.

Humiliated would probably best describe it. She did not know whether to laugh or cry.

She and Jimmy, a white haole boy, were taking an Asian Studies class that semester. There were other haoles in the class, but Jimmy was the only one who was proficient in Japanese. He had lived in Okinawa where his father, a colonel, was stationed.

When Jimmy discovered that she, Reiko, was from Okinawa, he began speaking Nihongo to her. She had heard other haoles in Okinawa speaking Nihongo, but Jimmy spoke it with hardly any American accent. He, of course, wanted to know how come she spoke English without a Japanese accent. She explained that her grandfather, on her father's side, was a Nisei born in Hawaii and had landed with the occupational forces as an interpreter during the Okinawan invasion. Her grandfather stayed on in Okinawa as a civilian worker after his discharge and married grandma, an Okinawan. One of the children was Reiko's father. He married an Okinawan also. An American citizen, he worked at the Air Force Base which enabled Reiko, also an American citizen, to attend American schools at the base.

"Maybe, you and I had gone to the same school," said Jimmy.

Maybe, thought Reiko, but not for long. After middle school at the base, Reiko attended a full-time Japanese school. Her mother wanted her to go to the University of the Ryukyus (Ryudai) someday. A university from where she herself had graduated. Which meant Reiko had to keep up her English studies at home. Her father, an English teacher at the base, made sure that her English home studies were the equivalent of the regular classes he taught.

"So. You must be very good in both Japanese and English." said Jimmy.

"My father wanted me to attend an American university someday," she explained. "Like he did."

"And you chose UH?"

"I have friends here."

"You sure made the right choice," said Jimmy.

And that was the beginning of a warm, but strange relationship. A young handsome haole boy interested in an Okinawan girl, who for the first time, was attracted to an American boy.

Jimmy was majoring in Asian Studies, minoring in music. He played the flute for the UH band, and was very good at it, sometimes performing solos at school concerts. He was also a good painter; some of his paintings were exhibited at the East West Center on campus.

Throughout their dating, if that's what it could be called, Jimmy's friend, Hitoshi, from Tokyo was always with them. Hitoshi, a musician and painter also, became a part of the inseparable threesome. Reiko felt fortunate that she was close not only to one boy, but two. One a haole, the other a Japanese. Both of whom very kind, sensitive artists, who took her wherever they went, concerts, plays, movies, football games, trips around the island. She couldn't tell who she liked better. Jimmy? Hitoshi?

This went on for a full semester and into the next.

Then!

She was alone with Jimmy in his car that night, riding up to Nuuanu Pali to see the bright night scenes down at windward Kaneohe. The wind, as expected, was blowing hard. They had stepped outside for a moment, looking down the steep cliff from the scenic Pali Lookout point, then had quickly returned to the car, their ears ringing.

They were sitting silently in the car, still looking out toward the faraway ocean and the sparkling shore lights, when Jimmy reached over for her hand. It was the most natural thing for him to do. Why did it take him so long?

"Reiko," he began, "you must know by now…"

She waited for him to go on.

"…We'll always be close, right?"

"Yes, of course…"

"You're the best… The best girlfriend I've ever had."

She held his hand tighter.

"But… Oh, Reiko… I shouldn't have let it go on this long…"

"Jimmy… What is it?"

"That's all we can ever be. Good friends."

She was puzzled.

"Reiko… You must've known…"

"Know what, Jimmy?"

"Me and Hitoshi… We're, you know…"

She waited for him to go on.

"More than just good friends."

She looked at him in the semi-darkness. His eyes were teary.

"Reiko… Hitoshi is my boyfriend. Y'know… My partner."

It finally came to her. Joltingly. Jimmy and Hitoshi!

"You understand what I'm trying to say?"

Dumbstruck!

They were always together. Jimmy, Hitoshi and her. Except for their classes together, she and Jimmy were seldom alone. And when they were, Jimmy, always warm, kind and lovable, never attempted to put his arm around her, or hold her hand, or give her an aloha hug. Never! It was because he was Jimmy, she had always told herself. He was a very sensitive, gentle boy who wouldn't take advantage of a foreign student away from home.

But…!

Goodness! Not Jimmy! Her closest friend in school. A haole Uchinanchu. Someone she really felt close to. Even loved.

"I didn't mean to lead you on," he now said. "I always want you to be my friend. You mean so much to me. More than a sister I never had. Especially an Uchinanchu sister."

Jimmy now wiped his eyes, words choking him.

"Please understand what I'm trying to say, Reiko."

Wiping her own eyes, she now held his hand in both of hers, reached over and kissed his cheek.

"I'm a very lucky girl to have a special friend like you, Jimmy."

For the first time, Jimmy put his arms around her and held her.

"...And I'm a very lucky guy to have a special friend like you, Reiko."

Yes, she thought now, fingering the petals of the leis she had around her neck. She brought up the pikake strand and inhaled deeply. The wonderful smell of the pikake and ginger flowers will always remain a part of her life.

Jimmy and Hitoshi had cut their classes to come to the airport and see her off. When they put the leis around her neck they hugged and kissed her.

"Aloha, Reiko," said Jimmy."

"Aloha, Jimmy."

"Sayonara, Reiko-san," said Hitoshi, bowing.

"Sayonara, Hitoshi-san," she said, bowing back, wiping her eyes.

After a whole year she was finally returning home. Well, actually, she had returned home several weeks before for Ojii-chan's funeral. The funeral was in Ie Jima, of course, at the family's grave where generations of Ojii-chan's ancestors were buried. The American forces had destroyed most of the graves during the invasion, but many of them were restored.

Ojii-chan had lived a full life. Over eighty when he died. He had been a high school teacher in the Motobu/Nago area, teaching English. His English wasn't great, but he had learned enough of it while hospitalized in an American POW camp to motivate him to go back to school and become an English teacher.

He had been in the Japanese Army and was wounded in the Ie Jima battle. He had lost his right leg, but never mentioned how he had lost it. Having been in a defeated Army did not make it a pleasant memory.

What made it so puzzling was why Ojii-chan chose to honor someone who invaded Ie Jima with the conquering forces.

She knew Ojii-chan had written something about the war, but did not share it with anyone. After many rewrites, he would place the writings in the family trunk, then would take them out, read them, destroy them, then would start all over. What he wrote about became an intriguing family mystery.

Now, at last, the mystery might be revealed.

After the funeral, before she returned to school, Obaa-chan grandmother had opened the trunk, taken out Ojii-chan's writings and had handed them to her.

"It was one of the last words Ojii-chan said before he died," said Obaa-chan, handing over the writings. "He said to give this to you."

Reiko had accepted the writings which were wrapped in a furoshiki silk cloth, and was tempted to unwrap them. But she had to catch the next plane to Honolulu. Even if she had brought the furoshiki with her, she wouldn't have been able to read its contents. Final exams were coming up. After that, she would be so wiped out she wouldn't have been able to devote her time to reading Ojii-chan's writings.

And so she left the furoshiki with Obaa-chan, telling her

that she would read them when she returned home in a few months.

The first thing she would do now when returning to visit Obaa-chan would be to take the furoshiki home and start reading Ojii-chan's writings. She had no idea what they were. Or why Ojii-chan wanted her to read them.

Chapter 3: Naha

Arriving at Naha Airport after a lengthy transfer from Narita Airport in Chiba Prefecture to Haneda in Tokyo, then to Naha, Chris, quite tired from the more than fifteen-hour flight, looked down sleepy-eyed at the evening scene down below. Naha seemed a large city not unlike Honolulu, the traffic lights just as congested, the multi-storied buildings brightly lit, other airplanes landing and taking off.

So. This is going to be his home for a year. The island of his ancestors, three generations removed. It was one hundred years ago that Grandpa left his homeland and sailed to an unknown chain of islands called Hawaii. It had taken almost a month from the time he left Naha Harbor, sailed up to Kobe and Yokohama, then finally to Hawaii Nei. And he, grandson Chris Tsugio, had made the same trip in less than a day.

Yeah, Grandpa, times have sure changed. You always dreamed of returning home wealthy, but could not even afford a trip home. You only went to the third grade in Japanese school, and could not read or write English, but your grandson is now a guest professor of the largest and most prestigious university in all Okinawa.

I'm here on your behalf, Grandpa. And I'll always be sure to tell everyone about your hard life here in Okinawa as well as the slave-like laborer that you became in Hawaii. And about your son, Tomoichi, my father, who joined the American Army and fought for his country in Europe during World War II.

The girl, Reiko, was now at a seat in the next aisle. She looked his way and nodded. He nodded back.

She had been a good company going to Tokyo. Talked a lot, but understandably inquisitive with a sharp mind. She'll most likely be in one of his classes. Hopefully, not too inquisitive and not too personal.

She waved to him and pointed down toward the airport. She was trying to say something which he could not understand, her mouth working silently.

He shook his head, pointing a finger at his head, indicating he did not know what she was saying.

She waved again. Then, finally, he could understand that she was saying she'll see him down at the terminal.

He nodded.

The terminal was as busy as the Honolulu airport, passengers rushing out of the custom lines as soon as they were permitted to pass, greeters waving and bowing, passengers in wheelchairs looking around, concerned that they had been forgotten, and the polite airport workers guiding long lines of tourists to their baggage.

Chris immediately saw Takashi Miyazato and his wife, Mariko, also a Ph.D out of UC Davis, whom he had met several times in California. They both spoke perfect English with hardly any accent, and were as American as anyone born and raised there.

After the welcoming greetings and making him feel as

though he had never left Honolulu, the Miyazatos helped claim his baggage and were directing him to their car parked nearby when the girl, Reiko, hurried over.

She, of course, knew Takashi and his wife.

She introduced her father to everyone, who also spoke flawless English, then her mother who greeted everyone in Nihongo. Both were about Chris' age, her father a little shorter and heavier.

Takashi was glad that Reiko, whom he had recommended to attend UH, had completed her year there, and would soon be graduating from Ryudai.

Reiko thanked Takashi profusely for the recommendation and giving her an opportunity to attend UH. Her father and mother joined in the gratefulness, bowing deeply.

The trip to Kina Mansion/apartment in the heart of downtown Naha did not take long. The apartment was next to the elevated Asato monorail station. It was a multistoried building with its office facing the monorail and the back entrance down a ramp into the garage.

Takashi and Mariko helped him register at the office, then helped him with the baggage to his apartment on the third floor.

He was pleasantly surprised when he stepped in. He had expected one of those tiny one-bedroom Japanese apartments he had heard of. The apartment had a kitchen, two bedrooms, a tatami matted living room with a TV, and a small bathroom with a toilet and a furo shower. The only furniture was the kitchen table with chairs and a double bed in one bedroom, a single bed in the other. Takashi suggested that he use one of the bedrooms as an office. As for cooking, he said it really wasn't necessary since the supermarkets nearby sold prepared lunch and dinner plates. Also, lots of fresh sashimi just off the fishing boats and fresh fruits and vegetables.

When he was finally alone, quite exhausted, he lay on the bed and tried to take a nap before going out for dinner. He could not fall asleep. Jet lag. Besides, he was still in Honolulu. Mentally. Thinking of Carrie. And trying not to think of Rose. That…!

Finally falling asleep and getting up hours later, he was too tired to go out for dinner. He lay in bed until falling asleep again. When he awoke hours later, the sun was up. Still jet lag.

Takashi came by quite early to take him to the university and to inform him about the bus route to the university.

Ryudai was on a hillside with several large campus buildings surrounded by wide expanses of green grass and tall semi-tropical trees.

His office, on the third floor, was couple of doors away from Takashi's. The office was much smaller than his office at UH. The scenery from the back window, however, was quite similar, the deep blue China Sea dazzling in the morning sun, the tropical breeze caressing the palm trees. Nearby, the garden of red and yellow roses was no different from those at the UH campus.

All the boxes of books, notes, photos of Carrie, and his laptop that he had shipped from Honolulu were already in the office. He quickly arranged the books on a shelf, placed the notes on another, then put Carrie's photo on the desk beside the phone. There was a time when Rose's photo would have been placed prominently on his desk, too. Before… Well, before she became a goddamn whore for a haole banker.

He e-mailed Carrie a short note. "Arrived safely. Settling down. Nice apartment. Nice campus. Students returning from a short semester break. Good time for you to come here is during your next semester break. I should be pretty familiar with the environs and the people by then, Dad."

At noon, Takashi came by and took him to the school cafeteria. Walking through the campus, he felt he indeed was in a foreign school. Back at UH the students were of every conceivable race, haole, black, Asians, multi-racial, tall, short, fat, some with shoes on, some with zoris, some bare feet, girls in shorts, boys in frayed Levis, T-shirt and, of course, Aloha shirts.

Here, the students were nearly 100% Asians, the exceptions being a few haole exchange students from the States. The students were dressed conservatively, everyone wearing shoes, everyone, of course, speaking Nihongo. A national university, nearly half of the students were from Mainland Japan.

He did not quite know what to expect at the cafeteria. Sandwiches? Hot dogs? Hamburgers? Lining up behind the students with a tray, he quickly discovered that the cafeteria was like an okazu ya restaurant back home. Rice, miso shiru, sashimi, chopped meat with vegetables, tofu, natto and crispy fried fish. Well, what do you know? Home away from home.

He could not distinguish the Mainland Japanese students from the local Okinawan students. They all spoke Nihongo Japanese, and all seemed relaxed and friendly. Growing up in Hawaii, he could almost distinguish an Okinawan from a Naicha non-Okinawan Japanese. Okinawans were a little shorter and almost always darker complexioned. Okinawans and the Naichas, of course, all spoke English. Both pidgin and non-pidgin English. Very seldom did anyone speak Nihongo.

As he and Takashi placed their trays on the table and sat down, the girl, Reiko, hurried over.

"Hello, Sensei," she greeted Takashi warmly. "May I join you and Yamashiro Sensei?"

"Hi, Kinjo-san. Sure. Of course. Join us."

"Hi, Reiko," Chris greeted. The girl seemed fully recovered from the journey, her warm friendly smile lovely as the day before.

"Ready to start another semester?" Takashi asked.

"Hai. Ready and eager."

"Good."

"I just found out that I'm the last student to register at Yamashiro sensei's American Lit class," said Reiko. "I was afraid there wasn't any more seats left."

"Word must've spread," Takashi said to Chris. "A famous professor from America lecturing a class here at Ryudai."

"Famous?" Chris said, chuckling.

"You're the author of two scholarly books, a playwright whose play was produced in Hawaii and here in Okinawa. Can't be more famous."

"Really?" said Reiko. "You had a play produced here in Okinawa?"

"Nothing great," he said.

"Directed by our famous director, Koki san," said Takashi.

"In English?"

Chris shook his head. "Translated into Japanese by him."

"Sensei. You never mentioned anything about it."

"I did. Some of the students did go to see the play."

"Oh, I wish I knew about it!"

"Maybe someday we'll have it shown again."

"That would be wonderful. I'll tell all my friends about it."

The sashimi was nice and fresh, the miso soup delicious, the fried fish as tasty as those in the Japanese-Hawaiian restaurants.

Takashi excused himself. He had a meeting to attend. He asked Reiko to take Chris on a tour of the campus: the law school, the medical school, the agricultural department and the English section of the library where Chris would be spending much of his time researching for his classes.

Reiko seemed quite popular on campus. Classmates coming up to her were glad that she had at last returned from Hawaii. There were also a couple of boys who, ignoring Chris, asked Reiko to go to a movie with them. Flattered, but not enthused, she rejected the boys politely, and turned to Chris. "We're all just friends," she said.

"Seem like nice boys," he said.

"That's the trouble," she said. "Just boys."

"No boyfriend yet?"

"Oh, I guess I did have one once. He became too serious."

"Playing the field, huh?" he said.

"Not really," she said. "Just don't want to be serious with anyone yet."

"You're still very young. I'm sure you'll meet someone before you're out of school."

"I hope so. I heard it's hard to meet someone after you're out of school.'

"Not for you," he said. "They'll still be men after you."

Flattered, smiling, she avoided his eyes.

The grand tour of the campus over, he invited her to his office where he opened the tiny refrigerator and brought out a couple of cold canned tea that Takashi had stored.

"Going back to Ie Jima soon?" he asked.

"I'll be going there this weekend with my mother and father," she replied. "To spend the night with Obaa-chan, my mother's mother."

"No Ojii-chan?"

"He died a few months ago."

"Oh."

"He had left something for me to read," said Reiko.

"Writings?"

She nodded.

"Had anything published?"

"Just in small magazines," she said.

"Have any idea what this one is about?" he inquired.

She shook her head. "I'm going to find out soon."

He looked at her.

"His gift to me."

"A legacy?"

"If that's what you call it."

"Should be interesting," he said. "A grandfather leaving his last writings to his granddaughter."

"Can you read Japanese?"

He shook his head. "Not even the simple words. Wish I had gone to Japanese school instead of going down to the beach on Saturdays."

"Maybe someday I'll translate Ojii-chan's writings, and show them to you. If you're interested, that is."

"I'm already interested. The unfolding of a mysterious man's life."

"Ojii-chan?"

"Any writings just before death is a mystery."

"Never thought about it that way."

"Maybe, you can use it as a class project. Y'know. A translation of an original manuscript. I'm sure you can get credit for it."

"Really?"

Chapter 4:
Ie Jima

That first weekend back home in Nishihara City near Ryudai, Reiko packed an overnight suitcase, put it in her five-year old Toyota, then helped her mother and father prepare for the two-hour ride to Motobu. There, she would drive the car aboard a ferry which would take forty-five minutes to cross the bay to Ie Jima island.

Passing by Kadena Air Base before taking the expressway, she remembered Kubasaki American High School on the base. After studying for a rigorous entrance examination for acceptance at a Japanese high school, she had transferred to a neighborhood Japanese school. Her mother's idea. Encouraged by her father. Her American high school education was continued by home study taught by her father.

She was glad she was able to graduate from the Japanese high school, which was much harder than her English home study courses. She had become quite proficient in Japanese and English and was finally accepted at the University of Hawaii as an exchange student during her senior year at Ryudai.

Thinking of UH, she wondered how Jimmy and Hitosh were doing. Jimmy. What an experience that was. A new world; a new kind of man. Of course, it was painful at first. She really loved him. Such a wonderful person. So tender, so kind, so warm, and so artistic. He had transformed her lonely stay at UH into a happy, learning year. She hoped he and Hitoshi would have a happy relationship.

The rest of the drive up to Motobu was colorful and spectacular as always. There were sakura cherry blossoms along the way, the seaside highway not as busy as during the weekday commuting traffic to Naha and cities down south.

As expected, there were many tourists at the Motobu dock, mostly Japanese from Mainland Japan and an elderly American couple, waiting to board the ferry. The ferry, quite big, one of the latest models, sailed toward Ie Jima, the pinnacle Gusuku Yama looming higher each minute. The ferry's TV was showing a baseball game in Japan and the young boys aboard were more absorbed in it than the scenery before them.

The ferry finally docked. The passengers began getting off eagerly with VCRs and cameras. Reiko and her parents waited for one of the dock workers to drive their car off the ferry. The late spring weather was a little hotter than the main island, no mountain breeze, no stirring of trees, the air sultry and humid, but not as oppressive as it would be in a few more weeks.

It was always so wonderful to be back on Ie Jima, Reiko thought, driving her car out of the harbor traffic and heading toward the flatlands of the island and to Iegusugu town. It wasn't too long ago when Ojii-chan would have been waiting for her at the dock. Those days were, of course, gone. Ojii-chan would no longer be there to greet her with open arms, nor would he ever be there to hold her hand and take her to the ice cream shop.

Ojii-chan... She fought back tears, maneuvering the car through a narrow village bridge. Ie Jima would never be same again. Not without Ojii-chan. Not without him taking her to the beach or going boat fishing. Or him taking her to the Ernie Pyle Memorial Park, pulling out weeds and raking leaves. And cleaning the plaque spotlessly shiny.

She wondered who is the caretaker of the Memorial Park now? It shouldn't be left unattended. Curious American tourists were always coming to the island, not so much as enjoying the ferry ride or climbing up the pinnacle, but to visit the Park. She could go there and carry on Ojii-chan's dedication. But how often would she be able to come to the island?

The elderly American couple aboard the ferry, she was sure, would go directly to the Park. They were at that age who would remember Ernie Pyle.

Obaa-chan Grandma, as expected, was waiting for them. Tears flooded her eyes as she greeted Reiko, bowing low. Reiko rushed up to her with open arms and hugged her. "Obaa-chan..."

Obaa-chan now returned the hug, wiping her eyes. "Genki de su ka, Rei chan? Are you fine?"

"Hai," she managed to say. "Genki de su. I am fine. Obaa-san mo? You, too?"

"Hai. Daijobu de su. I am very well."

Her mother and father, having been visiting Obaa-chan almost every weekend after Ojii-chan's passing, carried their overnights into the house. The house was a three-bedroom home with a tile roof, a water tank on it to store water from the rains and typhoons. It was a typical, compact island home, the steps of the front porch worn and frayed, the tatami-matted living room needing repair.

"Are you climbing up the mountain?" Obaa-chan wanted to know.

"You know I always do when I come here," said Reiko.

"And, of course, you'll be visiting Ojii-chan's park?"

"It wouldn't be Ie Jima for me if I did not."

After a brief moment, as they stepped toward the front steps, Obaa-chan turned to her. "Are you going to read Ojii-chan's writings while here?"

"I want to take them home, Obaa-chan. Then read them when I'm a little more settled."

"Please do, Reiko-chan. Ojii-chan said nothing about it to me, except that he wanted you to read it. He said now that you are older and a college student you would understand what was never explained to you before."

'Hai. I'm sure I will enjoy reading it, Obaa-chan."

"And please tell me all about it."

"Of course, I will, Obaa-chan."

"There were times when he wanted to talk about it, then would decide not to," Obaa-chan went on. "I know he went through a lot during the battles here, but like other soldiers who went through it did not want to talk about it."

"You really think it's about the war, Obaa-chan?"

"If it were anything else he would have told me about it."

So. That's what it's all about, Reiko told herself. What he went through in the war. It must have been less painful writing about it than talking about it.

After a light lunch of konbu seaweed, tako octopus, tofu, pickled vegetables and tea, they all went for a ride to the family ohaka. The grave was at the outer edge of the tiny village among other family graves.

Obaa-chan had brought along a plate of fried fish, tofu, and seaweed to offer Ojii-chan.

When the offerings were made, each of them bowed ceremoniously to Ojii-chan's spirit, burned osenko incense, and spoke quietly to Ojii-chan.

Wiping tears off her cheeks, Reiko told Ojii-chan that she missed him very much. That although he was with her in spirit, she missed his warm, smiling face and his calm comforting voice. For a second, Ojii-chan's image flashed before her and she choked back a burst of sobs. "Ojii-chan..."

Her father came over and put his arm around her. "You okay?"

She nodded.

'Miss him, huh?"

She nodded again.

"I wish I had been here with him during his last days," she said, covering her mouth.

"He went peacefully," said her father. "The way he wanted."

She nodded, although not entirely comforted.

"Rei-chan," said her mother, and spoke Nihongo, "you were Ojii-chan's favorite. "

"Even though I was not a boy he had wished for?"

"He was happy you are what you are."

"He couldn't have been closer to you, if you were a

boy," said her father in English.

Obaa-chan came over and held her hand. "Rei-chan, Ojii-chan had several grandsons, and he loved them all, but he was always partial to you."

She nodded gratefully.

In spirit, Ojii-chan's warm, smiling image flashed before her and she returned his smile.

Somewhat comforted, she drove everyone back to Obaa-chan's home. There, she cut a few branches of colorful roses from Obaa-chan's garden, put them in a vase with water, then took several osenko incense from Obaa-chan's obutsudan altar, and drove to the Memorial Park.

It was weeks ago that she had been there, since Ojii-chan's passing, and she was surprised that the expanse of green grass was well manicured, the weeds controlled, the brushes surrounding the park neatly trimmed. She wondered if the island leaders took it among themselves to maintain and preserve the park as Ojii-chan had done for years.

Parking the Toyota beside the white fence, she walked up to the plaque in the center of the park. The elderly American couple from the ferry was enjoying the colorful flowers inside the fence. They apparently had read the plaque and were now returning to it.

Reiko placed the roses on the stand above the plaque, burned a couple of osenkos and put them in a tiny ceramic ash container that Ojii-chan had grooved into the stand beside the plaque.

As she clasped her hands together in silent prayer, the American couple approached the plaque. They stood respectfully beside her, watched the ceremony, and said nothing.

Finally, the white-haired lady, most likely the wife of the elderly man, whispered quietly, "Wasn't Ernie Pyle a Christian?"

"I'm sure he was," said the elderly semi-bald man. "There's nothing in his life story says he was a Buddhist."

"Of course, he could have been converted," the lady said.

"Nah," said her husband. "From what I read about him, he wasn't partial to any religion."

Reiko at last turned to them. "Ernie Pyle-san was not a Buddhist," she tried to explain, "but the practice of burning osenko incense is not entirely a Buddhist rite."

"Ohmygoodness," said the lady, apologetically. "You speak English."

Reiko, having gone through this many times with Americans, smiled warmly. "I studied English in high school and college," she said simply.

"Here in Okinawa?" the lady asked.

"In Hawaii, too."

"Hawaii!" said the lady, "We were just there."

"We visited Ernie Pyle's grave at the military cemetery there," said the semi-bald man.

"The Buddhist burial must have been here and the Christian burial over there," said the lady.

Reiko wanted to explain that Okinawans' practice of ancestral worship was not Buddhism. She let it go.

"Why are you here going through this ceremony?" the man questioned.

"My grandfather started it years ago, and I'm just carrying on his wishes."

"Your grandfather? He knew Ernie Pyle?"

"Not really," said Reiko. "But he read enough about him that he felt he knew him."

"Same with Frank," the lady said. "He also was here when Ernie Pyle was killed."

"Here!" Reiko said. "On Ie Jima?"

"Not on this island," Frank said. "On the main island."

"But you knew about his death the day he was killed," said the lady.

"Not that day, Annie; the next day."

"All the way over in Okinawa?" Reiko said.

"Word spreads pretty fast among GIs," said Frank. "Especially about someone like Ernie Pyle. He was a friend of all of us. In Europe as well as here in the Pacific."

"Besides," said Annie, "Frank felt close to Ernie Pyle because he was from Indiana."

"A fellow Hoosier," Frank said.

"A fellow…?" said Reiko.

"Someone from Indiana," Frank explained. "He was born in Dana, not too far away from my hometown."

'You knew his family?" Reiko asked.

Frank shook his head. "But I've been to the Ernie Pyle museum in Dana. His whole life story is there. His writings, his correspondences, his war photos, his medals…"

"Where was that camp you were a medic?" Annie asked Frank.

"Eye-shi-ka-wa…"

"Know where that is?" Annie asked Reiko.

"Eye-shi-ka-wa…?"

"Used to be a Japanese POW camp."

"Oh!" said Reiko. "Ishikawa."

"Wasn't it also a camp for wounded POWs, too?" said Annie.

"That's why I was stationed there."

"Frank was in the medics," Annie said to Reiko. "He cared for our wounded as well as wounded POWs."

"Yeah. Just a young kid, barely knowing how to bandage a wound," said Frank.

"Oh, Frank," said Annie. "It gave you a good start. You wouldn't have gone to medical school without that experience."

"You're a doctor?" Reiko asked.

The man nodded. "Retired."

"It took him all these years to make up his mind to return to Okinawa."

"Aw, Annie… How many of us want to be reminded what we went through those days?"

"That was over 60 years ago, Dear."

"Like yesterday," said Frank, solemnly. "A nightmare. Watching men dying; watching young kids starving; mothers and daughters jumping off cliffs…"

"He saw more than the average soldier, because he was in the medical corps," said Annie. "There were times when he had to crawl into caves to care for our wounded. Tell her, Frank,"

"Annie! She wasn't even born then."

"She must've heard about the battles around here."

"Just a little," said Reiko. "Most of those involved are gone. Those still living don't care to talk about them."

"Hell, no," said Frank. "Why remind yourself of those days?"

"What about that young man you befriended, Frank? Y'know. That wounded POW who always thought he would be shot any day."

"Well, he wouldn't be a young man today."

"You said he spoke English."

"Just a little. Picked up more and more talking to us."

"What was his name, Frank. He might still be alive."

"He was my age, for Chrissake, Annie. What's his chances of him still being around?"

"Well, she might have... I'm sorry. You haven't told us your name."

"Reiko."

"Tell her that POW's name, Frank."

"Annie!"

"Okinawa isn't Indiana or Ohio," said Annie. "It's just a small island."

"There's still lots of people here."

"Aw, Frank."

Frank finally gave in. "I really never knew his real name. "It was Ken-itchey or something like that."

"Kennichi?" Reiko looked at Frank.

"Yeah. It was something like that. I ended up calling him 'Kenny.'"

"How badly was he wounded?" Reiko now stared at Frank.

"Pretty bad when they brought him. Still bleeding. Just

barely hanging in there. Never complained. Hardly moaned."

"And, he lived through it?" said Reiko.

"He was tough," said Frank.

"Where was he wounded?"

"He came in with one of his legs missing."

Reiko's hand jumped up to her mouth.

"You know who Frank is talking about?" Annie asked.

"My God!" Reiko's other hand jumped up to her mouth.

"You knew him?" Annie asked again, now her hand up to her mouth.

"You knew him?" Frank jumped in. "Kenny? You knew him?"

"Was his last name 'Oshiro'?"

Frank held his head sideways for a second, "Oshiro... Oshiro... That's it. Oshiro! Sounded like an Irish name."

"Ohmygod..." Reiko uttered. "That was my Ojii-chan."

"Your what?" Annie said.

"My grandfather..."

Both Annie and Frank cried out, "Your grandfather!"

Reiko burst out sobbing, her hands covering her mouth. This man knew Ojii-chan!

"Ohmygod..." said Annie.

"You're sure?" Frank said.

Reiko nodded. "My Ojii-chan lost his right leg in the war. Here at Ie Jima."

"Jesus!" said Frank. "You're right. Kenny's right leg was gone when they brought him in. He was hit here on Ie Jima. Same island Ernie Pyle got it."

All three stood there, silently, avoiding each other's eyes.

"I...can't believe it..." Reiko finally uttered. "You knew Ojii-chan."

"Well, yes and no," Frank said. "I mean we weren't buddies. We were still at war. Enemies."

But you treated him as a patient," Annie said.

"Of course."

Finally, somewhat recovered, Reiko said, "He hardly spoke of those days. But I remember him saying that instead of shooting him as he had expected, the Americans treated him quite well."

"He was wounded," Annie said.

"Jesus," Frank muttered. "Meeting the granddaughter of Kenny. –Where is he today?"

Reiko's eyes shifted away. "He passed away several weeks ago."

Silence.

"Can't expect any more miracles, I guess," said Frank.

"Frank, what about that carved cat? Tell her how you got it,"

"Lots of GIs and Marines brought home souvenirs," said Frank. "Y'know. Pistols, photos of Japanese families, flags, helmets... Some, even teeth of dead Japanese soldiers. "

"But you brought home a carved cat."

"I exchanged a pack of cigarettes for it," said Frank.

"A cat carved out of wood?" Reiko asked.

"POWs weren't supposed to have pocket knives. But nobody took it away from Kenny. It was just a tiny knife."

"The cat is beautiful," said Annie. "We've had it displayed in our living room all these years."

"Ojii-chan enjoyed carving animals," said Reiko. "His favorite was always a cat."

"It symbolizes peace, tranquility and contentment," said Annie. "A wise cat watching the rest of the world going through turmoil while he sits there in that lofty place minding his own business."

"Kenny was like that cat," said Frank. "Quiet, always minding his own business. Then, one day, he saw me reading the Stars and Stripes with a big picture of Ernie Pyle. He had seen other medics reading the news and wanted to know who that man was."

"I think Ojii-chan could already speak a little English at that time," said Reiko.

"Yes, he could," said Frank. "I gave him the paper and he sat up on his cot reading it. Took him a long time, but I could tell he was very interested in the article."

"I'm sure it's because they were both on that island," Annie said.

"He asked me who the man was," said Frank. "Why was everyone talking about him? I told him whatever I knew about Ernie Pyle then."

"We at home knew about our soldiers in battle reading Ernie Pyle's columns," said Annie.

"Kenny said nothing for the longest time," Frank said. "Then, he asked, "How?""

"We didn't know exactly how Ernie Pyle died at that time," said Frank. "All we knew was what the Stars and Stripes reported. That he had landed on that island with the GIs, and got caught in the line of fire."

"So sad," said Annie. "He wasn't a soldier. A reporter."

"Never carried a weapon," said Frank. "All he had was his pencil and paper."

"Ojii-chan must've liked Ernie-san, because he cared for the common soldier," Reiko said.

"For the underdog," said Frank. "Always for the common GI. A great man and a great reporter. There's been volumes of books written about his life."

"I've read some of them," said Reiko. "Ojii-chan ordered them from a bookstore in America. He kept up with anything written about Ernie-san."

"'San?'" said Frank. "Isn't that a way of showing great respect and honor?"

"Yes," said Reiko. "Ojii-chan always called him 'Ernie-san.'"

"Your grandfather might have known about Ernie Pyle's last day on that island," said Annie.

"How could he?" Frank said. "He didn't even know who Ernie Pyle was."

"Did he say anything to you about how he lost his leg?" Annie asked Reiko.

Reiko shook her head. "He never talked about the war."

"Annie," said Frank, "most of us who were in combat want to forget it."

"He could've kept a diary," Annie said to Frank. "Like you did."

"My diary covered the different islands we landed," said Frank. "Not about the actual fighting."

"My grandfather never talked about the war," Reiko

said, "but he could've written something about it."

"He could've?" said Frank.

"I don't really know what he wrote," said Reiko, "I haven't read it yet."

"Maybe he remembered you, Frank," Annie said.

"Aw, Annie," said Frank. "With all he went through why would he remember me?"

"You saved his life."

"Naw, I didn't. The guys who brought him in saved him."

"It's a shame that Ernie Pyle couldn't be saved," said Annie.

"The books I've read said Ernie Pyle was killed instantly by a single machine gun bullet," Reiko said.

"We've read that, too," said Annie.

"A single machine gun bullet…" Frank said, holding his head sideways. "Where did it come from? And why Ernie Pyle, a civilian?"

"Your grandfather might have known," said Annie.

"Aw, Annie."

"He was there, Frank."

"And so were thousands of other enemy soldiers."

"Will you be reading whatever your grandfather wrote soon?" Annie asked.

"I plan, too," said Reiko.

"Frank, give her your card so she can tell us about her grandfather's writings."

Frank reached into his back pocket for his wallet, dug out a card, and handed it to Reiko.

"I'd really appreciate it if you'd tell us what your

grandfather wrote," said Frank. "That is, if it's not too personal."

"Frank's mentioned about Kenny, your grandfather, several times after he returned from Okinawa," said Annie.

"I didn't get a chance to say goodbye to him that morning we were shipped down south," said Frank. "I hope he didn't think I had forgotten him."

Reiko looked at the card in her hand. "I'll write you and tell you what he had written as soon as I can," Reiko said.

"Yes, please," said Annie. "Your grandfather's been very close to us."

"Can't forget him," said Frank.

"How could we?" said Annie. "With that carved cat looking at us wherever we turn in our family room."

"You've kept it all these years?" Reiko said.

"It's a souvenir Frank treasures," said Annie.

"Are you in a hurry to return to the main island?" Reiko asked the doctor.

"Well, I'm not used to driving on the left side," said Dr. Sweeney. "Okay during the day; at night it's pretty risky."

"We drove all the way up from Naha," Annie said. "We better get back before dark."

"My Obaa-chan lives here in Ie Jima," Reiko said. "She'd be glad to meet you."

"Your...?" said Annie.

"My grandmother," Reiko said. "I'm here with my parents for the night."

Dr. Sweeney looked at Reiko. Calculating. "Is she about the same age as your grandfather?"

"A year younger," Reiko said.

"She must be the young girl who used to visit Kenney at the POW camp," Dr. Sweeney said.

"You met her?" Reiko said.

"Once," Dr. Sweeney said. "From a distance. She and other POW families used to hand food across the barbed wire fence. Kenny pointed to her and said she was a close friend."

"Frank," Annie said, "she might remember you."

"We just kinda nodded to each other," Frank said.

"Still…"

"Aw, Annie, that's sixty years ago."

"She lives only a few minutes from here," Reiko said.

"Frank!" Annie insisted.

Frank looked up at the sky, then westward toward the sun. "We won't miss our ferry, will we?"

"The next ferry won't leave for another hour," Reiko said.

"Frank," Annie said, "you did not get to see Kenny; you have a chance to meet his wife."

"Well…"

"Yes, Reiko," said Annie. "We'll be glad to meet your…?"

"Obaa-chan," Reiko said.

Reiko led them to her Toyota parked nearby and drove them to Obaa-chan's a few kilometers away.

Obaa-chan was alone in the front yard trimming the rose plants. She turned and looked curiously at Reiko who was approaching with an elderly American couple.

Understanding a little, but not able to speak English, Obaa-chan was speechless even in Japanese when Reiko introduced Dr. and Mrs. Sweeney and told her that she had actually met the doctor at the Ishikawa POW camp during the war.

The full impact of the introduction now registering, Obaa-chan's hand jumped up to her mouth, her eyes steady on the doctor. "He must be that American soldier who was kind to your Ojii-chan," she said, tears streaming down her face.

Reiko translated Obaa-chan's words.

"She remembers me!?" Dr. Sweeney said.

"Is she the same girl who was waiting for him to return home from the war?" Obaa-chan asked, indicating Annie.

"Hai," said Reiko. "They got married and he went on to school and became a doctor."

Obaa-chan bowed several respectful bows to Dr. and Mrs. Sweeney, and said to Reiko," Your Ojii-chan spoke of him several times." Looking heavenward, she said, "He must be very happy, your Ojii-chan, having his American friend marrying his girlfriend and becoming a doctor."

Reiko translated.

"He knew about us!?" Annie exclaimed.

"I must've told him," said Dr. Sweeney, winking at Reiko.

"What else did you tell him about us?" Annie said.

'Aw, Annie..."

"I know, I know," said Annie. "That was over sixty years ago."

"How many children do they have?" Obaa-chan asked Reiko.

Reiko translated.

"Three," Annie said. "And five grandchildren."

"Ah, so," Obaa-chan said, placing her hands together in a silent, blissful prayer when Reiko translated back.

"How about her?" Annie asked.

"They have five children and seven grandchildren," Reiko said.

"Good to hear that," Dr. Sweeney said. "Kenny lived a full life."

"Where did my father and mother go?" Reiko asked Obaa-chan.

"They went to visit their friends," said Obaa-chan.

"My parents, they're going to be disappointed not meeting you," Reiko said to the doctor and Annie.

"They've heard about Frank and your grandfather, too?" Annie asked.

"They'll know all about it when we tell them," Reiko said.

Bowing low, Obaa-chan invited everyone into her home for tea. But was told that the doctor and Mrs. Sweeney will have to be returning to Naha in a few minutes.

Obaa-chan excused herself and went into her home.

While Reiko was showing the rose garden to Dr. Sweeney and Annie, Obaa-chan came out with a pair of old wooden crutches. "Rei chan, ask the doctor if he remembers these crutches," she said, handing them to Reiko.

Reiko translated and turned the crutches over to Dr. Sweeney.

Dr. Sweeney gripped the crutches, studied them, staring at the initials on the upper arm of the crutches.

"My God!" he finally said. "He saved them all these years?"

"Then it was you!" said Reiko. "You gave Ojii-chan those crutches."

"See these initials," he said. "'J.M.' They belonged to one of our guys, Jim Michaels. Got shot on his upper thigh. Before he got transferred to the medical ship, he got himself metal crutches. He was about to throw these away when I saved them."

"And you gave them to Kenny?" Annie asked.

"He needed them," Dr. Sweeney said.

Obaa-chan turned to Reiko. "They reminded him of a very kind American soldier."

Reiko translated.

"Oh, Frank," Annie said, grasping Dr. Sweeney's arm affectionately, "you remember him by the cat he gave you and he remembered you by the crutches you gave him."

Reiko translated to Obaa-chan.

Again, bowing low, Obaa-chan thanked the American couple with tear-filled eyes.

And the American couple bowed back as best as they could.

Chapter 5: Ryudai

The first day of class. It was not just another first day of the semester like it used to be at UH. The students were all Japanese; not a single red- or brown- haired student among them. They, of course, all spoke Japanese among themselves. Quietly, politely, respectfully. They were all there to study and learn, their reverence for the classroom starting at the doorway. They, and he, too, took off their shoes before stepping into the rug-floored room.

He immediately noticed that the girls were seated up front while the boys were in the back, about evenly divided. At the very front row was Reiko, not as reserved as the others. Her eyes locked with his for a second and she nodded. He nodded back. Then quickly focused his eyes on his roster.

Twenty-five students, all seniors; all able to read, write and speak English. He had copied pages from "From Here To Eternity," which are what the class would be studying.

He handed Reiko the pages and asked her to pass them to the rest of the class.

Wasting no time, Chris introduced himself. "I'm Chris Yamashiro. Professor of American Literature from the University of Hawaii. I have all of your names here in my roster. Please give me a few days to get to know you.

"I am an Uchinanchu like most of you," he went on. "My grandfather and grandmother came from Yambaru."

The class laughed. Some, however, remained straight-faced.

"Oh, by the way, how many of you are from Mainland Japan?"

Three boys and two girls raised their hands.

"Naichi, eh?" Chris said.

Again, the class, except for the Mainland students, laughed.

Chris turned to Reiko. "That's insulting?"

Reiko shook her head. "But we don't refer to them as 'Naichis.'"

"Oh?"

"Just, 'Mainland Nihonjins.'"

"What about 'Yambaru?'"

"It refers to the mountains or countryside."

"Well, that's where my family came from. They were Yambaras."

The class laughed again.

"I'm a sansei," he now said. "Y'know, Third generation Japanese. Or third generation Okinawan from Hawaii.

"I guess that means nothing to you. Your ancestors go back far beyond that.

"Anyway, this class is an American Literature class. If you're here trying to learn Japanese Literature, you're in the wrong room. I can't even read or speak first-grade Japanese."

The class politely refrained from laughing out loud.

"How many of you have heard of the American book,

"From Here To Eternity?"

Most of the class raised their hands.

'In Japanese or in English?"

"In Japanese and in English," said the girl beside Reiko.

"How about the rest of you?"

"In English," said the rest of the class.

"Good. As you know, the story takes place in Hawaii just before World War II and during the first weeks after the war started. How many of you have been to Hawaii?"

Half of the class raised their hands.

"Did you go to Pearl Harbor?" he asked.

No response.

"Why not?"

One of the boys raised his hand. "I did not want Americans to stare at me and blame me for the attack," he said.

Chris sympathized and understood. He himself had never been to Pearl Harbor, much less visit the SS Arizona sunk there. He would have been uncomfortable hearing the hundreds of haole white tourists condemning the attack and staring at him.

"The rest of you will feel you've been to Hawaii and visited Pearl Harbor before this class is over, " he said.

"How many of you have been to Mainland Japan?"

Every hand went up.

"How many of you visited the Emperor's palace?"

Three girls raised their hands.

"The rest of you have never been to the palace grounds?"

"Why go there?" said the boy who had gone to Hawaii.

"It's where your Emperor lives."

"There are other places to visit in Tokyo," the boy said.

He was surprised that most of the class hardly expressed any reverence for their Emperor.

"How many of you know all the words to 'Kimigayo?'" he tested.

One girl in the back raised her hand.

"You mean the rest of you don't know the words to your own national anthem?"

"Why know it?" said the same boy.

"To honor and respect your Emperor?"

Reiko raised her hand. "The elders blame the Emperor for the thousands of Uchinanchus killed during the war," she said. "And the young people have heard about it from them."

Chris had been sure the students would express their devotion and affection for their Emperor.

It's a new Japan, he told himself. Democracy at work. He had heard that in the old days everyone bowed low and did not dare look up whenever the Emperor rode his white horse before his subjects. Violation of this law and order could have one's neck chopped.

He now assigned each student the section of "Eternity" that he or she had received. Starting next week, the student would read that section in class and everyone would openly participate in a class discussion.

He referred to the class roster and had the student tell him what section he or she had.

"Right now," he went on, "as I call your name, please stand and tell us a little about yourself."

"In Japanese?" a girl asked.

"If you want me to know what you're saying," he said, chuckling, "you'll have to speak English. As a matter of fact, I would appreciate very much all of you speaking only English the moment you step into this class."

A murmur spread among the students.

"Sensei," a long-haired boy addressed, "all right I ask question?"

"Sure. Go ahead."

"You say you Japanese, but cannot understand Japanese?"

He shook his head. "Sorry. I can't."

"How come?"

"I grew up speaking English."

"Even to father; mother?"

"My father and mother were Niseis. Second generation. They spoke English to me."

"Only English?"

"Oh, sometimes, a little Japanese mixed with Hawaiian," he said. "We call it Pidgin English back in Hawaii.

"Any more questions?"

Reiko raised her hand. "Maybe, Sensei, you should explain what is Pidgin English."

'You want to know?" he asked the class.

"Yes!" they all responded.

"Well, first of all you have to understand that Hawaii is made up of many different races, Japanese, Chinese, Koreans, Filipinos, Portuguese, Irish. Even Germans and Swedes.

"The first generation were all foreigners. They spoke their own language among themselves. When they spoke to other foreigners, they mixed their own language with whatever English they knew.

"So… What they spoke was a mixed-up English. Or what we call Pidgin English."

"Why call it 'Pidgin?'" the boy wanted to know.

Chris was stymied.

Reiko came to the rescue. "Pigeon is a bird," she said. "They are all over the world. And they make funny sounds. Like laughing or crying. And so when the first Portuguese came to Hawaii, all the foreigners speaking together sounded like the pigeons back home in Portugal."

"So, Pidgin English is Portuguese?" said the boy.

Chris chuckled.

"That's what my Portuguese friend in Hawaii told me," said Reiko, keeping a straight face.

"Well," said Chris, "that's as good an explanation as any."

"So," said another boy, "your father and mother, dey speak Portuguese to you?"

He looked at Reiko.

"No," said Reiko, coming to his rescue again, "Pidgin English is not Portuguese."

"But you said…"

"It sounds like a bunch if pigeons all speaking at once," she said.

Still puzzled, the boy said, "Oh…"

"Okay," said Chris, "now that that's settled…"

"Give us example of Pidgin English," a girl up front requested.

"Well…" He hesitated, trying to recall a good example.

Christ! He grew up speaking Pidgin. "Okinawan Pidgin," he finally said. 'Oi, Ojii-san, you, today, hana hana sabitan?' That's Japanese, English, Hawaiian and Okinawan…"

"Don' sound like Pidgin."

Oh, for chrissake.

He looked over at Reiko again. She shrugged helplessly.

"Okay," he said, ignoring the boy, "when we meet for our next class, that's two days from today, we'll start with our "From Here To Eternity" discussion. The first one will be…, (he checked his roster) "Shinzato, Chiyoko." He looked around the class until one of the girls raised her hand. "Oh, there you are. So, Shinzato-san, please be ready."

"Hai, Sensei."

"The rest of you, please start preparing for your own presentation. Okay?"

"Okay, Sensei!"

He let the class go over their sections while he went through the roster, memorizing the names and faces of each student. Back at UH it was Harry, James, William, Edward… Here it was Hisashi, Tadashi, Taichi, Urara… Oh, God…

What a difference, he thought, between the students at University of Hawaii and the kids here at University of the Ryukyus. The Japanese kids there and here all looked alike. The similarity, however, ended there.

What was hard for the kids here was to grasp that the Japanese-American kids back home were constantly reminded that "You are Americans; not Japanese. Learn to speak proper English!"

He, like other kids in Hawaii grew up speaking Pidgin. Speaking proper English sounded phony. As though imitating the haole white kids. Even today it's perceived that way. Especially among the boys.

For him, it was a little different. His father, a country boy growing up in a Kailua pig farm, learned a harsh lesson during his Army days in Mainland U.S. and in Europe. There were quite a few Niseis in his outfit from California, and they could not understand him. He got in a couple of scraps with them when he thought they were "making fun" of him. "What did you say? Are you speaking Japanese? What's that word again?" He thought they were a bunch of sissies. Mahus.

It was only during the combat days in Italy, France and Germany that he learned the Mainland Japanese boys were as tough as the bullies from Hawaii. Many of them won the Distinguished Service Cross, one of them the first Nisei to be awarded the Medal of Honor, posthumously.

When Dad came back from the war, collecting disability checks for his million-dollar wounds sustained in France, he was a changed man. No longer the pig farmer's son from Kailua. His best buddy in the hospital was a fellow Nisei soldier from Oregon, who, of course, spoke proper English. His buddy intended to continue his college education on the GI Bill of Rights to become an architect. When asked what he intended to do with his GI Bill, Dad really did not have an answer. Surely, he had no intention of carrying on his father's pig farm. And so he replied without really meaning it that he was going to UH to become a schoolteacher.

His buddy reminded him that he'd better speak better English to his students.

"Ah…"

But that remark made Dad aware that if he wanted to become a schoolteacher he'd have to start speaking proper English.

And that's when Dad started his crusade to speak better English and forget Japanese as well as Pidgin. Going to UH made it easier. Although the students spoke Pidgin among themselves, they were very capable of speaking proper English in class discussions.

Dad eventually got his Master's and became a principal of a country grade school on the Windward side of Oahu. And mom, a schoolteacher there, eventually became his wife.

Chris now wished he had listened to Mom and had gone to afternoon and Saturday Japanese classes. "There was nothing wrong with learning Japanese," she had said. "This is America," Dad had argued, "not Japan." And so he had sided with Dad and ignored Mom's pleading. For which he regretted. Mom was right. "What's wrong with learning Japanese? The war against Japan was over."

He was sure he'd learn Japanese, both speaking and writing, if he applied himself during the year he'd spend in Okinawa. But that wasn't his real goal. He wanted to learn more about his grandparents' homeland. What made them leave? Migrate to a place they knew nothing about? Didn't they miss their homeland? Their parents? Their sisters and brothers?

Whatever, he was glad he did come here. The sabbatical

would do him a helluva good. Especially now that the divorce proceedings are in the hands of his and Rose's attorney. Why punish himself listening to Rose's diatribe. That's a nice word, "diatribe." Describes Rose perfectly.

When the bell rang signaling the end of class, the students went to the doorway, put on their shoes and went to their next class. Except Reiko.

"I'm sorry if I confused the class," she apologized.

"I'm sure they understand perfectly well what 'Pidgin English' is all about," he said, laughing.

She joined his laughter.

"Did you go up to Ie Jima over the weekend?" he asked.

She nodded. "I returned with Ojii-chan's Chronicle."

"What's it all about?"

"His life during and after the war."

"Rough?"

She nodded. Solemnly.

"I told Professor Miyazato what you told me. He thinks you can get credit for the translation."

"It's not going to be easy," she said. "It was painful just reading what Ojii-chan went through."

"The best writings," he said, "evoke strong emotions."

"I don't know how he kept it to himself all those years."

"How long will it take you to do the translation?"

"I'll have to really understand what Ojii-chan is trying to say before I start."

He reached over and patted her shoulder. "I'm sure you'll do a good job."

Chapter 6:
The Translation

Late that evening, Reiko began rereading Ojii-chan's Chronicle. Wanting to be sure that she won't be disturbed by telephone calls or hear her father and mother talking, she locked herself in her bedroom sanctuary.

The Chronicle was over a hundred pages. All, of course, written in Nihongo. She had gone through them twice before, but felt she had missed some of Ojii-chan's spiritual and philosophical expressions. Ojii-chan, she knew, could read English. He had sometimes combined English and Japanese meanings, making it difficult for her to really absorb what he had tried to say.

Her plan now was to read the Chronicle once more, all of it, then go back to page one and start the translation. She did not know how long it would take to finish the entire Chronicle. She must, however, be sure to capture Ojii-san's spiritual aim in writing his Chronicle.

It was past midnight when she finally came to the last page. Again, she had to fight herself from bursting into sobs. "Oh, Ojii-chan. Poor Ojii-chan. Keeping all this to himself all those tortuous years."

While still caught up in an emotional roller coaster, she went back to the first page. She would start right now. Like anything else it was the beginning that was the hardest.

She knew the Chronicle so well now, after reading it three times, she could almost recite passages from it. Can she do it in English? Replace the delicate and intricate Japanese words with English words and phrases without losing the flow of Ojii-chan's deep meanings?

The Chronicle was divided into three sections: (1) A Young Boy; (2) A young Man; and, (3) An Old Man.

With pen in hand, a Japanese-English dictionary and a blank pad before her on the desk, she read the first paragraph and began writing in English:

Rei-chan, I knew that someday I would be telling you all this. By then I'm sure you will be old enough to understand why I waited all these years to tell you.

From the time you were a little girl, Rei-chan, I always enjoyed having you beside me. I always enjoyed holding your hand and walking around our neighborhood or walking down to the beach and feeling the sand under our feet. But the most enjoyable moments were when you and I walked around Ernie-san's park, pulling the weeds, raking the leaves and trimming the trees.

You were too young to ask me why we were always at Ernie-san's park. It was enough for you, and for me, that we were spending the beautiful days together at the park. Someday, I always told myself, when you are old enough, I'd like to tell the story of me and Ernie-san.

And now is the proper time.

You, see, Rei-chan, I did not really know Ernie-san while he was still alive.

It all began when the war with America started in 1941. I was a young barefoot boy on Ie Jima, enjoying a happy, carefree, island life. Maybe, too happy; maybe too carefree. Little did I realize that the war would one day come to Okinawa and to Ie Jima.

I was only 14 years old then. Not quite aware what was going on away from our island. Some of our older boys were joining the Army or Navy right after high school and were sent to faraway places I never heard of, Guadalcanal, Sumatra, Borneo, New Guinea.

I was going to high school near Motobu at that time. We did not have one here in Ie Jima. I would come home during the weekends then sail back on Sunday nights. It was the most wonderful time of my life. And I hoped it would go on this way forever. But, then, Rei-chan, wonderful things don't last forever. It is an interlude in one's life which can only be best described as a dream.

In late 1944, when I was seventeen years old, many soldiers from mainland Japan started arriving on our island. We all looked up to them. The mighty soldiers were our protectors; our saviors.

We quickly noticed that their spoken Japanese was much superior than ours. They did not have our Uchinanchu accent. They spoke as though they were all from Tokyo. We finally had a chance to learn about life in a big city.

It was about that time that the Americans first bombed Okinawa. Naha City was beginning to be destroyed and other places like the Kerama Islands were heavily bombed. We could see faraway smoke rising from the destructions, and were glad the Americans were not bombing Ie Jima. Why would they? There was nothing important here.

Let me tell you about those Japanese soldiers, Rei-chan. At first, they were kind and considerate. When the Americans started the bombing and shelling of Okinawa and an invasion by American troops was close, the Japanese soldiers began hating us. They blamed us for the bombing and the threat of an invasion by the Americans. If we spoke our Uchinaguchi language, which was often, they accused us of being spies for the Americans. An Uchinanchu old man was killed for speaking Uchinaguchi. And he did not even know how to speak Nihongo!

By now, I, too, was in the Army. I went through a brief training period in Motobu, learning how to shoot a rifle and a machine gun, then was sent back to Ie Jima. We all became busy digging trenches and building machine gun concrete fortresses all over the island. Mt. Gusuku was the most fortified place on the island. There were artilleries and machine guns aimed at all parts of the beaches from the pinnacle.

Our instructions from the high command were to let the Americans land safely, giving them the impression that there were no Japanese soldiers on Ie Jima, then when they felt secure and safe, we would open fire and kill as many of them as we can.

Every Japanese soldier in Okinawa and the surrounding islands was instructed to kill at least one American soldier before he himself was killed. And so that became our goal. Kill at least one American soldier before we, too, were killed.

My unit was stationed at a machine gun concrete fort facing Motobu. There were six of us. We expected the main

American forces to land from Motobu. And we were ready. We would be able to carry out our orders and sacrifice ourselves for the glory of the Emperor. Tennoheika Banzai!

The Japanese soldiers, I noticed now, were becoming less concerned for us Uchinanchus. They began killing our chickens, ducks, pigs and cows for their own food supply. We did not dare complain. We were told it was for the war effort and that everyone must make sacrifices for the Emperor.

The bombing on Okinawa island were becoming worse each day. Early one morning, at sunrise, when I looked across the bay toward the center of Okinawa and toward Naha, I was shocked. There were hundreds, maybe thousands, of ships assembling and landing troops. At first, very hopefully, I believed they were Japanese ships who had come to rescue Okinawa from an American invasion.

I could not have been more wrong. They were all American ships! Battleships, aircraft carriers, destroyers, cruisers, landing crafts as far as you could see. And thousands of smaller crafts going from the big ships to shore, all transporting American troops. And in the air were hundreds, maybe thousands, of American airplanes protecting their troops. Where were the Japanese battleships and airplanes?

That was the morning of April 1, 1945. How can I ever forget that day!

Reiko's eyes were now heavy. It had taken three hours to read the Chronicle and now over an hour to write five pages. She laid the pen on the pad and looked over at the clock: 4:00 A.M. She did not have a class until 10:00 A.M.

She placed her head on her forearm and shut her eyes.

Waking up a few minutes later, she began reading the Chronicle again. The translation would take longer than she had thought. She counted the Chronicle pages she had completed. Fifteen. She knew she had cut down some of the Japanese words and sentences in translating them. She hoped she did not diminish Ojii-chan's intentions. Some of them were poetic; some flowery; some difficult to replace with English words. All she could do was to picture Ojii-chan before her, telling her how he wanted the words said in English.

The beginning of the Chronicle, she knew, was to prepare for the revelation at the end. And it was the revelation that motivated her to keep translating on. Ojii-chan, she realized, had written his Chronicle into a novel form: beginning, middle and a climactic ending. It was now up to her to translate it so that it seemed like a novel more than a Chronicle.

She picked up the pen and resumed writing.

In our concrete fort, the five Japanese soldiers, all older than I, missed their homes. They were not from Tokyo. They were from small villages all over Japan. One was from a tiny village in cold, freezing Hokkaido. Another was from Shikoku island. The others were from the outskirts of Hiroshima, Kagoshima and Fukuoka. The sergeant in charge of our unit, a career soldier, had fought in Manchuria and China. A fanatic, the sergeant belittled us constantly, especially me an Okinawan. The Army, he said, must be terribly desperate to have an Okinawan serve in the same unit with veterans like him. Okinawans, he claimed, did not have the required dedication, loyalty and courage to fight the enemy.

As I listened to the sergeant's mockery of Okinawan soldiers, I was determined to show him that I am a loyal Japanese, just as loyal as he, perhaps even more, since I was there defending my island. In the Army, however, a low recruit did not dare speak back to his superiors. The sergeant, being a sergeant, was someone who was to be obeyed loyally and his judgment never questioned.

The fighting in central Okinawa, we were told, was fierce and costly. When the Americans first landed they had thought the island had been abandoned. The Americans were not met by fanatical oppositions. Instead, they landed as though welcomed. It was then that the Japanese forces who had concealed themselves in caves, trenches and hillsides, suddenly appeared everywhere and charged the invaders.

Banzai! Banzai! Banzai!

Ushijima Taisho, the Commanding General in Okinawa, had planned the counterattack and was successful in inflicting heavy American casualties. Japanese soldiers all over Okinawa were ordered to carry on the same tactics.

And here on Ie Jima we were determined to surprise the invading forces and drive them back to the sea.

Reiko's eyes were again getting heavy. She rubbed them. It was now 5:00 A.M. She'd go to bed until 9:00 A.M., get up and head for her 10:00 A.M. history class. Then, maybe, go to Professor Yamashiro's office. Tell him that she had started the translation and was very happy with it so far.

"Professor Yamashiro?" He had told her to call him, "Chris" on the airplane coming from Hawaii. It wouldn't be proper to call him that in his classroom. She'd keep addressing him as "Professor Yamashiro" when among the other students, and "Chris" when they were alone.

Chapter 7:
The Invasion

Later that night, Reiko, after studying for her history class, went back to Ojii-chan's Chronicle. She first re-read what she had translated, made a few corrections, then went on translating.

Distracted, she thought of her visit to Chris' apartment and was glad he had enjoyed her goya champuru. She wondered if he thought she was bold and daring going to his apartment. An unescorted young girl visiting a man's home in the evening! Well, why shouldn't she? He was alone and lonely and needed company.

He was so different from other professors, she thought. Always smiling that warm, attractive smile of his and laughing heartily. Never making himself seem important. Always treating her and her fellow students as though they were his friends or his peers.

Of course, she had an advantage over the other students. She had, after all, spent nearly a whole day on the plane with him. And he had spoken intimately with her about his life and his goals.

Oh, Reiko! Just because you sat next to him on the plane doesn't make you someone special. But he did say things to her that she was sure he wouldn't have said to anyone else. About his daughter and his wife. About his studies at UCLA; his trips in California, Oregon and Washington

State.

Oh, stop it, Reiko! You're just another student of his. Besides, he's happily married. To a very successful business woman.

She tossed her thoughts of Chris aside and began the translation. She heard Ojii-chan speaking to her.

Rei-chan, wars are terrible. Its only purpose is to kill and annihilate a fellow human being. Our unit waited for the moment to carry out our goal. To kill as many barbaric Americans as we could before they killed us.

Six of us, scared and nervous, waited for the moment to open fire. We could see them landing from their small crafts, looking around them, ready to fire their rifles. We could tell that they were surprised there were still no one firing at them. Only a few minutes more, we told ourselves. Just a few more minutes! You Americans will soon find out.

By now there were countless of them scattered on the beach front. They, like us all young, were eager to fire their rifles or machine guns. Unlike us, however, they were much taller, much bigger than us. It did not matter. Wars are won by soldiers who are willing to die for what they believed in, not by their size.

We kept holding our fire. The Americans kept advancing less carefully, lowering their guns, some of them smoking cigarettes, chewing gum, saying something funny and laughing.

The big machine gun pillbox to the right of us was led by Sergeant Morikawa. We looked at him, waiting for his signal to open fire. He kept studying the advancing Americans. When is he giving us our signal? When they are right on top of us?

Suddenly, with no warning, no signalling, we heard the Sergeant's machine guns firing up front at the unsuspecting

Americans. Our corporal, not waiting another second, opened fire, too. Our machine gun and the Sergeant's machine guns were firing so rapidly we could not hear ourselves screaming at the Americans who were either been shot or dropping down on the sand.

We kept firing. I kept supplying more and more belts of machine gun bullets to the corporal and the crew, yelling and screaming and cursing the Americans for landing on our island.

I don't know how long we kept it up. The Americans by now knew where we were. They kept firing their rifles in our direction which did not matter. Our thick concrete walls kept protecting us.

I had just taken a step back to gather more bullets when one of the enemy's artillery shells landed on our roof. Then another! I was tossed aside against the back wall like a bag of rice.

I could not believe I was still alive. The pain in the bottom half of my body was tortuous! I must still be alive to be able to feel it, I told myself. I reached down. One leg was still there. The other was dangling loosely. Blood was flowing down my forehead into my eyes.

Everything before me was blurred.

I looked around. The rest of my unit, all five of them, were not moving. Most likely all dead.

I crawled over to the machine gun, which was tossed against the wall. I looked up through the opening and could barely see the Americans maneuvering to the left and right of me, sure that they had killed us all. In terrible pain, I crawled over to the machine gun and managed to straighten it. I directed it out through the window.

It was so quiet now I was sure death was awaiting me. I could not die. I have not killed an American yet. I must kill an American before I die!

I waited for the enemy to appear before me.

No one came.

The pain in my dangling leg was so unbearable I knew I could not last much longer. It was like a slow-burning fire frying the flesh in my bone.

I thought I heard a truck approaching the road before me. It was one of those small American vehicles, a jeep. I gathered all my strength and shifted the machine gun in that direction. I wiped the blood off my eyes. I made sure my vision was not playing tricks on me. When the jeep came into direct site of my machine gun, I pulled the trigger.

I looked up front, the jeep was empty. The soldiers had jumped out and were hiding in the ditch along the dirt road.

I had missed my mark.

I wiped the blood off my eyes again.

I could see a head out of the ditch.

This is the moment I have been waiting for! To carry out my duty of killing an American before I died.

Just as I pulled the trigger, I heard Sergeant Morikawa's machine guns going off.

In that split second, the American rifles and machine guns opened fire on me.

A lifetime later, I opened my eyes. I looked around. I was not dead. The pain in where my right leg used to be was now barely noticeable. I was on a stretcher being transported to a landing craft at the beach.

The barbarians had saved my life! To execute me later.

Why? Why are they sparing me? They, I was sure, had

applied a pain killer to the stump of my dangling leg. I could hardly feel anything there. Kill me! Kill me! You barbarians.!

When I regained consciousness, I found myself in Ishikawa, at a POW medical camp. I gathered all this after talking to a wounded Nihonjin POW on the goza mat next to mine. He, too, wondered why the Americans had saved his life. It was a trick. They wanted information from us. About how heavily Ie Jima was fortified. About where were the rest of the machine gun forts.

I kept wondering when are the barbarians going to torture us! Burn us alive!

The days stretched into weeks; the weeks into a month. I was still at Ishikawa POW camp. Now a one-legged POW. A half-a-man.

Ashamed and disgraced for not dying a brave death, I kept to myself. The other POWs seemed adjusted to their new lives. They seemed resigned to: "Shikata ga nai. It couldn't be helped. What will be will be."

I did not feel that way. I had betrayed my loyalty oath. I had failed to kill a single American. And now I was a humiliated prisoner of theirs. If there had been a grenade near me, I would have pulled the pin and ended my shameful life.

Reiko raised her head away from the Chronicle. Poor Ojii-chan. How he must've suffered.

She could not imagine Ojii-chan ever hating anyone. Or wanting to end his life because he had failed to carry out "Yamato Damashii."

She had looked up the term in her dictionary: The spirit and soul of Japan.

She went on translating.

And now I had to put up with these barbaric Americans.

Gaman. To persevere; to endure.

Reiko did not want to stop the rhythmic flow. That was the hardest part of it all. To project herself into Ojii-chan's spirit and forget herself and not let her own words interfere with the flow.

I was still waiting for the Americans to take me away from the others and start their torture, Ojii-chan went on. *The other wounded POWs seemed more relaxed and trusting as the weeks went by. They had abandoned their spirit of Yamato Damashii.*

I still could not trust the easygoing Americans. The cigarettes and chocolate they offered us were now their weapons. To bribe us into disclosing how many Japanese soldiers were in Ie Jima, Motobu and Nago. To help them capture more of us. To tell our soldiers that the Americans are kind and gentle and forgiving.

I, of course, did not believe any of that. The Americans, when looking at a POW like me, felt triumphantly superior to us. They could have killed me instead of sparing me. They could have left me rotting in the machine gun pillbox for the rats and ants to eat me alive. Instead, they wanted to show me how kind and concerned they are of their enemies. They treated my wounds, brought me to a field hospital, and helped me recuperate. All for the sake of torturing me later for vital information.

Well, they are not getting information from me. They will have to burn me over their wooden stove and let me cry for mercy. They still won't get it.

I don't know how they discovered that us POWs somehow loved to eat American canned food like pork and beans, spam and so-called C-rations. And, of course, pots of rice. I was determined not to become a victim of their trickery.

I refused to eat. I would starve myself to death before revealing whatever information they wanted from me. But hunger and starvation, like lack of sleep, can drive you out of your mind. They are stronger than torture. The smell of canned spam cooked on a frying pan became stronger than my will not to eat any damn American food. Once I tasted the fried spam cooked with soy sauce, I could not stop myself. I had never tasted anything so delicious! It melted in my mouth. And the rice that went with it made it even more delicious.

One of the American guards who seemed concerned that I was starving myself to death, said, "It's up to you, man. You wanna die from starvation, it's your goddamn business." Of course, I did not understand what he said at that time, but now that I'm able to speak and understand English quite well, I'm sure that's what he said.

When that guard saw me eating the spam and rice, and the pork and beans, he tried not to care one way or the other. But I caught him smiling when he turned away.

That guard's name was Frank. I never found out his last name. He couldn't pronounce Kennichi. So he called me Kenny. I tried to tell him that I am a Nipponjin; not an American. He said, "Right now, you're Kenny to me". He was the conqueror; he could call me whatever he wanted.

Frank, my age, was anything but a typical American soldier. He was not angry at me or the other POWs for killing his GI friends. He just wanted the war to end so he could go home. No different from all of us. Except, in our case, we now had no home to go back to.

Frank did not smoke, I noticed. I did. And so whenever he had cigarettes with his rations, he would give them to me. Funny about human beings. You could tell without really trying to find out if someone is sincere or tricky. Frank, I could tell, was not a typical loud American looking down on the rest of the world. I could tell he felt almost guilty guarding us and treating our wounds. He seemed the type who wished everyone was nice and friendly without any hatred.

The other guards, I could tell, did not share his feelings. They hated us. They called us Japs, gooks, slant-eyes, sonsofabitches... I had never heard Frank use those words. I got so used to him calling me Kenny that I began calling him Franky.

One day, he brought me a tree branch and told me to make myself a crutch. Imagine that? An American whose duty was to kill me now helping me to get well. It did not take me long to carve a crutch with it. I had a small pocket knife that I had hidden in my pocket, and none of the guards seemed to mind me possessing it.

I had kept a part of the branch, and began carving a cat out of it. Now that I had only one leg and could not do many of the other things I used to do, I thought I better do things I could do. And carving was one of those things.

The battle of Okinawa was now concentrated in the South where Ushijima Taisho was willing to fight to the last man. I don't know how many of our soldiers had been killed by now. From what I heard there were nearly 100,000 soldiers in the area. All willing to die with the Yamato Damashii spirit. For Tennoheika. Although I still had that spirit, it was no longer as strong as it had been. Like Franky I wished the war would end soon, the killings stopped.

Franky told me a little sadly that he, too, would be sent to the battlefields in the South soon. He was in the medics, and there would be hundreds of wounded American soldiers needing medical care. If he were lucky, he said, the Japanese soldiers would realize it was senseless to continue fighting when they knew they would be defeated. I could not explain to him that Japanese soldiers are different from American soldiers. That we wished to die in battle rather than staying alive as a POW. Had I not been wounded, I, too, would have fought to the end.

Now look at me. A helpless soldier.

By now, I had heard of a famous American in the GI newspaper. I gathered that the man was loved by the GIs. He was not a soldier; he was a newspaper correspondent who died in Okinawa.

It was the first time that I noticed Franky bitter, angry and outraged. I, of course, knew nothing about the newspaper correspondent. "Why would anyone want to kill him!" Franky screamed. "He wasn't even carrying a rifle. He was just covering a war story."

Franky showed me a photograph in the newspaper. It was a photo of a middle-aged man, lying on the ground, lifeless.

"Ernie Pyle was the best friend us GIs had," Franky said. "He was with the Army in North Africa, Italy, France and Germany. He even landed with the Army in the Normandy invasion. He informed the people back home what was going on in the front. Everybody in America read Ernie Pyle's columns. About the horrors of war. Of young American boys dying in the battlefields. He wrote about us common GIs; not about the generals and admirals and the higher-ups. He was always for the underdogs, not for those bastards in Washington who never saw a day of combat."

The newspaper reporter must've been a great man to have risked his life to tell the Americans about life in the battlefields, I thought. He must've been loved by all the common soldiers if how Franky feels about him is any indication.

Reiko laid her pen on the desk, lowered her head, and took a deep breath.

She must write Dr. Sweeney, Reiko told herself. Tell him that Ojii-chan remembered him very well. About how much Ojii-chan appreciated Dr. Sweeney's kindness. And how Dr. Sweeney had introduced him to the world of Ernie Pyle.

Right now the flow and energy and rhythm urged her to go on with the translation. She knew her translation was going along quite well. She'd better not stop.

After all the big battles Ernie Pyle had been through, said Franky, he had to be killed on a tiny island no one's heard of.

What tiny island? I wondered.

He didn't have to be right up there with the GIs, Franky continued. The other reporters stayed back at headquarters writing their stories from what they heard. Not Ernie Pyle. He had to see for himself. Feel what it is to be fired upon. Share the fear and risk that us GIs are going through.

I compared this man, Ernie Pyle, with our own war reporters. Our reporters never wrote about us common soldiers; always about the generals and admirals and the leaders back in Tokyo. Medals of Honor were given to our generals and admirals who were made heroes by the newspapers.

I sure like to get my hands on that sonofabitch who shot Ernie Pyle, Franky added.

As the days went by, I could hear the other guards talking about Ernie Pyle. They mentioned all the battlefields that Ernie Pyle had been through and his newspaper reports about the common GIs. It seemed Ernie Pyle was now a martyr among the GIs and all the Americans back in America.

I began wondering about this humble man who touched the hearts and minds of everyone. He was a humanitarian; not a warrior. He was willing to sacrifice his life for his fellow Americans in the battlefields as well as for his readers back home in America.

There were many common Japanese soldiers who were heroes, but never heard of, because the newspaper reporters were not willing to write about their heroism. The common soldier was not good news.

The Japanese newspapers did not have reporters like Ernie Pyle who believed and cared for the low-ranking common sailors and soldiers. It was they who did the fighting; not the high-ranking officers who stayed behind in their nice, clean headquarters, and urged those under them to fight and die for the Emperor with the spirit of Yamato Damashii.

At 18, I began aging rapidly. Wars! So senseless! So wasteful! Is this what life is all about? To kill or be killed? To hate or be hated? To maim or wound or to be maimed or wounded?

I thought of all the Japanese war stories in our history books glorifying wars and their great conquests. And now this. The total destruction of a nation and its people at the mercy of a much superior enemy.

Reiko had to look up several Japanese words in the dictionary to write their English version. She was glad that Ojii-chan wrote as simply as he could. Otherwise, she'd be looking up every other word.

It was now ten o'clock. She'd have to get up early, prepare a bento lunch basket for her and Chris, nigiri rice balls covered with seaweed, pickled turnips, dried squids and a container of hot ocha tea. On their way to Mabuni they could stop and visit some of the deep caves that were used for hospitals during the war.

She was sure he'd enjoy the trip. And she would enjoy showing him the various historical sights.

Chapter 8: Mabuni

Early next morning, Chris was waiting eagerly for Reiko at his apartment. So far, he had not seen anything significant in Okinawa. Just the crowded cities, the university campus and the shiny blue sea. This was the island of his ancestors. Yet he knew nothing about it. Had not even seen the historical sites he had read about.

He had, of course, read about the battles of Okinawa, and had seen pictures of the destructions. But they had all been impersonal. Something that happened 60 years ago to people he could barely identify with.

It was hard to believe that the kids in his classroom were the children of grandparents who had gone through the pain and suffering of the war. Talking to them, he could not detect any bitterness or hatred toward the presence of American troops on their island.

On the other hand, it was the Americans who had helped start the university, he found out. Not only in Japanese; in English also.

There was a knock on the door.

He stepped over and opened it.

"Hi," Reiko greeted with her usual warm smile that was always on the edge of a laughter. "Are you ready?"

"Ready and eager."

"I'm parked downstairs in the driveway. The guard

said it's okay as long as I was right back."

He followed her to the elevator, taking in her slim figure in a tight-fitting Levis, her hair rolled up with a ribbon. A college student out of the UH campus. Even her slippers were Hawaiian.

In the third-floor elevator, he could smell her soft pikake perfume. No doubt from Hawaii. Her white silk blouse was neatly pressed, her front protruding slightly.

She thanked the guard, got in the Toyota on the driver's side which was on the right, waited for him to get in, then started out of the steep driveway into the heavy traffic full of motor bikes, bicycles and horn-blowing taxis.

Driving on the left side of the street, she made a sharp turn away from Kokusai Dori, the Broadway of Naha, and headed down the main highway near the ocean. She made another sharp left which confused Chris for a second, not quite used to sitting up front and riding on the driver's left.

They were out of the city in a few minutes heading south, away from the city's crowded and noisy traffic. Out in the open narrow two lane highway, he felt he was in windward Oahu away from Honolulu. Kailua, Kaneohe, Laie, Kahuku... Unlike Oahu, however, there were no sky-reaching mountain peaks, only a continuous range of lush, rolling green hills.

Reiko drove silently for a few minutes after pointing out the various scenic spots. Then, "Are you listening to me, Professor Yamashiro?"

"Oh, yeah. Sure, Ms. Kinjo."

She laughed. "You can call me, 'Reiko.'"

"Really?"

"Really."

They both laughed.

It was long drive to Mabuni. They drove through narrow village streets, winding two-lane country roads, China Sea to the right, the Pacific visible at certain points to the left, and the skies a bright glaring blue. Unlike Hawaii, the humidity at this time of the year was already muggy and sticky.

They now came to acres of lush green rolling hillsides and rows and rows of fertile vegetable fields.

"Must be good soil," Chris said.

Reiko turned to him a second, then looked up front. "A great big gravesite," she said with a tinge of pain.

"Gravesite?"

She nodded. "It's soil from the skeletons and bones of soldiers who died in this area during the war."

He looked at her.

"There were thousands of bodies all over here during the last days of the war. No one was left to bury them."

"They were just left there?"

She nodded.

"And they became part of the soil?

"Expensive fertilizer," she said.

He remained silent. So did she.

They finally rounded the last hilly bend to Mabuni, the valley suddenly spread out before them in a great wide expanse of highly planned and magnificently-arranged landscape. There were acres upon acres of green, well-manicured grass leading up to rows upon rows of black granite memorial slabs. They were like the Vietnam

Memorial slabs in Washington, D.C. Only in a much grandeur scale.

Directly ahead was a huge structure which Reiko pointed out was the prefectural museum. To the left of was another huge structure its high tower pointing skyward. It was the peace tower, according to Reiko.

Chris had heard about Mabuni and its holy grounds dedicated to world peace, but had not imagined the extent of its true magnificence.

They parked and walked over toward the coast line of the China Sea. Before them was a gigantic water-sprouting fountain, an eternal flame shooting skyward in the center. They then stepped over to the memorial walls which were spread over acres of green lawn.

Reiko, who apparently had brought other tourists here, explained that there are over 249,000 names on the walls. In one section, she said, are the names of Americans soldiers and Marines who died in Okinawa.

"American service men?" he said.

"The names of everyone who were victims of the war," said Reiko. "Most of them Okinawan men, women, children, and of course, Japanese soldiers."

Chris shook his head. 249,000!

"And more who were wounded in the war are added each year," Reiko went on.

Ahead, at one of the granite rocks, was a family placing flowers on the ground level, burning osenko incense and praying and mourning privately.

Chris had heard from his father and mother that they had relatives who perished in the war. He wondered if they, too, were part of the walls. He should have found out their names. They were, after all, his relatives. Three generations removed. He'd have to write to mom and find out their names. Ironically, he suddenly wanted to know more about his ancestors who died in the Okinawan battles.

The whole Mabuni area was peaceful and sacred, people walking around quietly, silently, respecting the rich, deeply meaningful surroundings. Despite its magnificence, however, Chris kept feeling a deeper depression gripping him. Until now, the battle of Okinawa was something that took place in the distant past and was an impersonal and historical past. Now however... 249,000! Some of them, who knows? His cousins; his uncles and aunties; his ancestors.

All for what?

Suddenly, his students at Ryudai meant more to him than just college kids. Their grandfathers and grandmothers were all survivors of the deadly war.

The museum did not relieve the depression that began at the granite walls. There were accounts of horrors committed by Japanese soldiers on Okinawan civilians. They were afraid the Okinawans would turn against them.

The Peace Tower, a few minutes away, finally did bring some relief. As they entered the huge ornate building with its tall, sky reaching tower there were children singing soothing Japanese songs. Songs that reminded him of his own childhood.

The children, Reiko explained, were grade school students from mainland Japan who came to Mabuni every year by the busloads. They came to commemorate the brave Okinawan students who had sacrificed themselves for the Emperor.

Ahead, before them, loomed a gigantic, sparkling statute of Buddha, it's head nearly touching the three-story ceiling.

"It was made by Okinawa's most famous sculptor," Reiko said. "Yamada Sensei. It took him 20 years to finish it."

"It's the biggest statue of Buddha I've ever seen," Chris said, awed.

"It's not a statue of Buddha," said Reiko. "It's a statue of peace."

"Oh?"

"It's the only statue in the world made entirely of lacquer."

"Not bronze?"

"Pure Okinawan lacquer."

He looked up the huge statue, at its delicate eyes, its classical nose, its firm fingers folded together, convinced now that it certainly must have taken at least 20 years to build it.

Although not a particularly keen observer of fine Oriental paintings, he glanced around the big circular room and could not help but marvel at the colorful paintings. Until now, he had never associated paintings with Okinawans. Okinawans, he always believed, were like the native Hawaiians, enjoying home-made alcohol and playing samisens and ukuleles.

He now noticed Reiko speaking to a middle-aged man

at the entrance. They seemed to be friends. When Chris passed them and went on to the next painting, Reiko stopped him. "Chris," she said, "this is Higa-san the administrator of the Peace Memorial."

After shaking hands, Higa-san invited Reiko and Chris into a room for special guests.

The room was not especially big, nor spacious, but it contained a long table with rich colorful chairs around it. Higa-san explained that when Emperor Akihito came to Okinawa and visited the peace hall, he was invited into this room.

And he had sat at one of the chairs covered with colorful red silk cloth.

Chris, not really serious, but not wanting to let the moment go by, asked Higa-san if it was all right for him to sit in the chair. Higa-san, caught off guard, looked at Chris, then broke off in soft laughter. "Sure," he said. "Go ahead."

Chris sat in the chair, head high, regally, and assumed a position of a head of state.

Reiko laughed. So did Higa-san.

Chris, joining in the laughter, felt a trifle foolish, yet appreciating the significance of the moment. Him, a grandson of an uneducated Okinawan pig raiser in Hawaii, sitting in the same chair that the Emperor of Japan had sat.

Chapter 9: Kudaku Island

It was now noon. Reiko decided to drive over to the Pacific Rim then up to the Chinen Peninsula. She wanted to show Chris a famous site not known to outsiders, Sefa Utaki.

At the Rim, she drove up a narrow winding road, the blue, dazzling ocean below more spectacular each minute. There were several cars parked wherever there was an open space at the top.

Chris had been rather quiet after leaving Mabuni, maybe exhausted from the long ride or maybe emotionally exhausted after seeing all the names on the memorial granite rocks. He seemed to have enjoyed, however, sitting on the Emperor's chair at the Peace Museum and had her take several photos of him.

Now at Sefa Utaki, Reiko wondered how he would take to participating in an Okinawan ritual. She knew nothing of his religious beliefs or background. Was he a Buddhist? A Christian? Being an intellect, he was sure to be interested in the beliefs of his Okinawan ancestors.

They came to a huge slab of rocks dripping water into a small pond.

"This is Sefa Utaki," she said, indicating the slabs of rock that formed a tunnel. "Uchinanchus come here to pray."

"Here?" Chris asked. "To these rocks?"

"Not to these rocks," she quickly said, leading him through the tunnel. "To an island."

"They pray to an island?"

She nodded.

"You, too?"

She did not nod nor shake her head.

At the end of the tunnel was a large opening. Several worshippers were standing there praying silently with beads wrapped around their wrists. Before them, on a rock table, were food and money offerings. They continued praying silently to a tiny island miles away.

Reiko stepped over to the offering table, placed a yen bill on it, and wrapped her hands together in silent prayer.

She motioned Chris to do the same.

Chris politely refused to do so.

She did not insist. It's a belief completely strange to him, she told herself. Even though he was a fellow Uchinanchu.

"That's Kudaka Shima," she said, pointing to the distant isle. "According to legend, the first Okinawan king and kami-sama god lived there for many years. The spirit of the Sun God brought great people to Kudaka Shima from faraway oceans."

Chris stood there, nodding silently.

Did he believe what she just said? Or just listening politely?

"Want to go on a boat ride to the island?" she asked. "It's still too early to drive back to Naha."

He looked at his watch.

"It takes only a few minutes."

"Sounds like a good idea," he said. "The ocean breeze should be nice."

In twenty minutes, they were down at Azama, a small port town with scuba diving outfits and excursion sail boats. It was a part of a tiny, quiet, lazy village, no one in a hurry. Even the young girl in the office did not seem to care if they were in there to go on a boat ride or to escape the outside heat wave.

They were the only passengers on a small boat slightly bigger than a fishing boat. They sat in small, mildewed, folding canvas chairs, watching the wharf gradually fading in the back, the brackish water below them churning from the boat's motors.

She began snapping photos of beautiful Chinen Peninsula, concentrating on Sunrise Chinen Hotel where they had stopped for soda pop before going on to the wharf. The boat began to rock a bit as they headed out to the open sea toward Kudaka.

There were several small islands to the left and right, some inhabited, others just sitting there in the bright sunlight surrounded by the peaceful sea. On one of the islands were several tourists, most likely from Mainland Japan, enjoying the isolation and perhaps dreaming that they were the only ones in the world.

Ahead, Kudaka Shima grew bigger. There was hardly an inch of elevation to the island. Just a long stretch of sand bars. No hills, no cliffs, no tall trees. She remembered flying over Kahoolawe Island when flying to the big island of Hawaii once. Although uninhabited, Kahoolawe, like

Kudaka Shima, was also a sacred isle, according to the native Hawaiians.

They finally entered the breakwaters; then to the island's tiny harbor. Several fishing boats were moored to the makeshift terminals. The harbor seemed deserted. The captain expertly angled the boat against the side of the terminal.

No taxis beckoned for riders. Everyone was minding his own business. No one greeted or invited you into a shop or a restaurant. So different from the main island where you're hustled the moment you look into a store window.

Climbing up a steep hill from the wharf, they finally noticed a middle-aged, semi-bald man, standing beside a shiny Honda van. Dressed casually with his shirttail out, he smiled-laughed at them, his greeting sign. He immediately recognized Chris as a gaijin foreigner.

Reiko asked the man if he was a taxi driver. The man said there were no taxis on the island. But he was glad to take them around the island as a courtesy. The man, obviously not able to speak English, addressed himself only to Reiko. He claimed he was the foremost historian of Kudaka Shima and would gladly take them around to places rarely seen by outsiders.

The man's name was Uchima-san.

They got into Uchima-san's van and started looking for the rarely seen places. Reiko hoped Uchima-san would stop smoking.

His van not only reeked of cigarette smoke, but the entire inside seemed stained with smoke. She was tempted to open the window. It was either getting lung cancer or having the outside heat wave get to you. She opted for the second-hand smoke. The heat wave was immediate; the cancer gradual.

She was hoping Uchima-san would take them to all the mysterious spiritual sites she had heard of. Uchima-san stopped along the shore and led them up a trail. Instead of following the trail into the forest, he halted and said this was as far as they could go. Only authorized women and priestesses were allowed further in. He pointed to the far end of the trail, not daring to step any closer. That is where the priestesses hold their ceremonies, he said.

"What ceremonies?" Chris asked, understanding a little of Uchima-san's Nihongo.

Uchima-san turned to Reiko. "Only women on the islands know."

"Oh?" said Chris, suspiciously.

Uchima-san drove through various parts of the isle, never more than a mile away. Chris was getting impatient. Whenever they came to a place of interest and he wanted to see more of it, Uchima-san said only priestesses were allowed there.

Reiko, of course, knew about the superiority of women over men in traditional Okinawan religion. Only women were allowed to enter sacred precincts. Men were not only forbidden from participating in the rituals; they were not even allowed to enter the sacred sanctuaries.

They finally came to an open space where several miniature temples were alive with burning osenkos. This must be the place they have been looking for, Reiko told herself. They got off the van and inhaled much needed fresh air. Second-hand smoke have not gotten to them yet.

Uchima-san, standing against one of the temples, took out a brand new pack of cigarettes from his shirt pocket and pounded it expertly into his open palm. He fingered out one of the cigarettes, stuck it between his thick, tobacco-stained lips, lit up and filled his lungs with smoke. If he's heard of lung cancer the moment's pleasure overshadowed it.

Reiko, still patient, held back a chuckle when thinking of their tour guide. All he's done up until now was to drive them around the tiny island, barely half of it, and telling them they can't go there, they can't go here, they can go there but not beyond the rock markers. And always warning not to take anything when they left the island, rocks, shells, wood, sand… You do, you will have bachi punishment from the Kudaku Shima's spirits who will follow you wherever you go.

Reiko immediately kicked off the sand sticking to her shoes, and dropped a leaf she had snapped from a tree branch a moment ago. She didn't really believe in such superstitions, but you just can't tell.

Chris had been looking into a long cage beside a smoke house. He suddenly jumped aside.

"What's wrong?" Reiko asked.

"Stay away from there," Chris warned, moving farther away.

Reiko, curious, stepped up to the cage. There were hundreds of tiny snakes crawling all over inside. She began snapping photos of them.

Uchima-san gave out another of his smiling-laughing

response. "Sea snakes," he said.

"Whattahell they doing in there?" Chris said.

Uchima-san was amused. "Kudaka Shima is very famous for them," he said.

"Famous?

"Medicine."

"People eat them?

"They are cooked in there first," Uchima-san said, pointing to the smoke house. "Then they are sent all over Okinawa. Even to Mainland Japan.

"Cheap ones are 3,000 yen," he went on. "Better ones are 10,000 yen."

"That's over $30 to $100 for each for those slimy things!"

Uchima-san stepped closer to Chris and said softly, "It is medicine for men who have hard time getting it up."

Reiko heard what Uchima-san said. She pretended not to have understood.

"Uchima-san," she said, "do we still have noros and yutas on Kudaka Shima?"

Uchima-san took a hissing breath between his teeth, his head held sideways. "The noro we had on Kudaka moved to the main island," he said. "There are people in need of her over there."

"What about Yutas?"

"Yuta? Yes. We still have one more remaining here."

"Can you take me to meet her?"

"Well...," Uchima-san said, "I'll have to talk to her first."

"Where is she?" Reiko asked.

"At my home," Uchima-san said.

"Your home?"

"She's my wife."

"Your wife is a Yuta?"

Uchima-san nodded, smiling-laughing.

"What's a Yuta?" Chris asked.

"She's a…powerful woman. She can see the future and predict many things," Reiko said.

"Like what?" Chris wanted to know.

"Typhoons, earthquakes, deaths," explained Reiko. "She can also predict your future and advise you which is the best road to take. If you're a woman and about to marry she can advise you if the man is the right man."

"Or, if the woman is the right woman?" countered Chris.

"Yes, of course," said Reiko.

"Uchima-san," she said, "when can we see the Yuta, your wife?"

"Come," said Uchima-san, "my home is that house over there," and led them to a small wooden structure with a faded tile roof.

Approaching his home through a narrow, grass bordered trail, Uchima-san called out, "Shigeko! You have someone to see you!"

In a second, a woman, Uchima-san's age, in a casual kimono, her hair combed back in a bun, appeared at the front porch. She greeted them with Uchima-san's laughter and smile. Unlike Uchimai-san the lady bowed a low respectful bow, then looked directly into Reiko's and Chris' eyes.

"You are here to visit me?" said the lady.

"Hai," said Reiko. "I've heard about the Yutas on Kudaka island but have never met one."

The Yuta smiled-laughed a warm greeting.

"Both of you?" she asked.

Reiko looked at Chris. "Want to?"

Chris took a step back. "You go ahead."

"Gaijin?" the Yuta asked.

"Hai. Hawaii kara."

"Ah, so. Hawaii." The Yuta bowed to Chris.

Chris bowed back politely.

In a moment, Reiko climbed up the front steps and was led into a semi-dark room. She looked around, surprised that there were no unusual decorations, mysterious ornaments or photos. It was a quiet room with cushions around a low table. In the middle of the table was a candle burning softly.

The Yuta invited Reiko to sit across from her.

Reiko, quite excited, sat down on her cushion, her hands folded on her lap, trying to remain calm.

"You are from Okinawa island?" the Yuta asked.

"Hai.

"And your name is…?

"Kinjo, Reiko."

"From Naha?"

"Hai."

"It must be nice to get away from all those noisy cars and people," said the Yuta.

"It's never nice and quiet like here in Kudaka Island," said Reiko.

"I visited Naha once," said the Yuta. "I never went back."

The Yuta now reached over and held Reiko's hand. "You are a seito at Ryudai?" she asked.

Reiko was surprised. How could she know that she was a student at the university? Then she realized that on the top right corner of her blouse was printed University of the Ryukyus.

"You are taking your gaijin friend to visit our islands?" the Yuta asked.

"Hai."

"He seems to be a gentleman," said the Yuta.

"He is one of my professors at the university," said Reiko.

"You are interested in him?"

"Yes. As my professor."

"Is he interested in you?"

"As a student of his," said Reiko.

"You see him as a father figure; are you sure he sees you only as his student?" the Yuta questioned.

"Yes, course," said Reiko. This is getting ridiculous, she thought.

"Do you know his background?"

"He is a happily married man and has a daughter who just graduated from college."

"Did he say he was happily married?"

"Well… No, he didn't say it. But…"

"Then, you don't know whether he is happily married," said the Yuta.

"Yes, he is," Reiko insisted.

"If he is happily married, what is he doing here in Okinawa without his wife?" said the Yuta.

"He's here as an exchange professor."

"And left his wife behind?"

"I'm sure that was their agreement," said Reiko.

"Has he said anything wonderful about his wife?"

"Well…"

"You should ask him," the Yuta said.

"Ask him if he is happily married." Reiko said.

"Ask him what he thinks of you."

"What he thinks of me."

"Reiko-san, there is nothing wrong with liking your professor."

"Please," Reiko said, "I want to talk to you about other matters."

"Like?"

"My Ojii-chan's Chronicle. Am I translating it like he wants me to?"

The Yuta rubbed Reiko's hand warmly, mumbling something sacred to herself.

"Your Ojii-chan was a great man," she finally said. "He saw and went through many tragedies in his lifetime which made him a caring and compassionate man. In doing your translation, you should become your Ojii-chan and let him do his own translation."

"He is no longer with us," said Reiko.

"Yes, he is," said the Yuta. "If you concentrate hard enough you will forget who you are and you will become him."

"Ojii-chan?"

"His spirit is all around you. Open your heart and your mind and he will become a part of you."

"Did Ojii-chan suffer a lot because of what he did?" Reiko asked.

"For any other man, what he did was just another event in his life," said the Yuta. "For your Ojii-chan, being a sensitive, spiritual man, he could not forgive himself."

"Poor Ojii-chan…" Reiko muttered.

"Life is full of tragedies, Reiko-san. Some of us learn from them; some of us repeat them."

"Ojii-chan wanted forgiveness. Did he get it?"

"If he searched for eternal forgiveness, he received it; if his search was just for a moment, it led to more suffering."

Reiko sat there in silence for a moment, analyzing her conversation with the Yuta. Has she really said something to her that was a revelation? Everything seemed general. Nothing specific. Except, of course, Chris and her situation. Situation! It was anything but a situation. Just a… The Yuta was wrong. Chris and she were just… Well, just good friends. Of course, she liked him. As someone whose company she enjoyed. Very much. But… Beyond that? Of course not. Why, he's old enough to be her father.

Is Chris really not happy about his marriage? she asked herself. Of course, she couldn't ask him. That'd be crossing the line.

When the session was over, she insisted that the Yuta accept a token of 3,000 yen for her enlightening information. For just $30 it was worth every penny.

Waiting patiently, Chris and Uchima-san were enjoying the air conditioned van. Uchima-san asked Reiko if she learned much from his Yuta wife. Reiko said that his wife was very insightful and taught her much about her own life. She found herself avoiding Chris's eyes.

At the wharf Chris insisted that Uchima-san accept the 5,000 yen for his grand tour of Kudaka island.

"Ah, that is too much," Uchima-san said, hand extended, laughing-smiling. "You are very generous."

"It's too bad that we were not able to see those secret places where only the Priestesses are allowed," said Reiko."

"Next time I'll take you there," Uchima-san said.

"To those forbidden places?" said Reiko.

Uchima-san laughed-smiled, and stuck the money in his pocket.

Chris laughed. "Money has power on this island, too, huh?" he said.

Uchima-san continued laughing-smiling.

"Please thank your wife for the valuable information she gave me," Reiko said, again avoiding Chris' eyes.

Chapter 10: Pig Feet Soup

It was nightfall when Chris and Reiko finally arrived back in Naha. They had talked about their day-long trip to Mabuni, Sefa Utaki, Chinen Peninsula and Kudaka Island, and thought it was a day well spent. About half an hour before nearing Kokusai Dori, close to Chris' apartment, Chris had shut his eyes for a moment.

"Chris," he heard Reiko awakening him. "You're home."

He opened his eyes, surprised that he had fallen asleep.

'I really dozed off, huh?" he said, chuckling.

"You must be tired," said Reiko. "We covered a lot of ground."

"Yeah, we sure did. Hey," he said, "are you in a hurry?"

"Well… I'd like to do some homework."

"It's Saturday. No school tomorrow. Let's go to this place on Kokusai, a special place I found. Authentic Okinawan food."

Reiko laughed. "You are in Okinawa, Chris."

"I know, I know… But this place serves pigs feet soup."

"So does lots of other places."

"They can't beat this place, Kokusai Miyako. The best pigs-feet soup I ever ate. Almost as good as my grandmother's back in the Kailua days."

Reiko thought it over for a second. "I guess I can do my homework tomorrow."

"Leave your car here," he said. "We'll walk over."

"What about the guard?"

"This space is for guests. And you're my guest tonight."

He stepped toward the garage. "C'mon upstairs for a minute. I want to see if I have an e-mail from back home."

Upstairs, Chris opened the door and let Reiko in. "There's orange and pineapple juice in the refrigerator," he said, stepping into the converted bedroom office. "Help yourself while I check my computer."

The computer screen showed several e-mails, one of them from his attorney Douglas in Hawaii. He clicked it to Douglas' e mail and waited anxiously for the words to appear.

Hi, Chris, it began. Had a long talk with Rose this morning. Bad news. She had her bank appraiser go over to Kailua and appraise the farmland. The seven acres are worth at least $500,000, according to the report. It's right in the middle of a major home development that's coming up. She wants half of it. Do we fight her? Settle? Compromise? Or initiate a nasty divorce case accusing her of, among other things, infidelity?

"Douglas?"

Chris read the mail again, controlling himself. Howdahell could she do that, appraising the property when she knows damn well he won't give in? So she did put in some of her own money to improve the property? Ten thousand at most. If that much. On the other hand, he was willing to give her the right to their home, no strings attached. Jesus! His share of their home is worth far more than a quarter of a million! And he's willing to hand it all to her.

He printed out the mail. Read it again. Then, unable to control himself, squashed the sheet of paper and threw it against the computer. "Damn bitch!" he shouted, then quickly realized that Reiko was in the next room.

"What's wrong, Chris?" Reiko said, stepping into the office.

"Huh? Oh, nothing. Nothing."

"Something wrong with your family?"

"Oh, no. Nothing like that. It's just... You ready to go? Did you have some juice?"

"I had a sip of your pineapple juice. Really sweet."

"Good. Glad you liked it. C'mon. Let's walk over to Kokusai."

Outside, they headed down the semi-dark alley, through a narrow side street, then finally came to brilliantly lit horn-blasting and motorcycle roaring Kokusai Dori. For a moment, just for a moment, back in the alley, Reiko reached for his arm then quickly let go.

"Are you sure you don't want to be alone?" Reiko now asked, breaking the silence. "We can go to that restaurant some other time."

"Right now is a good time," he said.

They finally came to the door of a small upstairs restaurant with an English sign "Kokusai Miyako."

"I know why you like this place," Reiko teased. "You can read the sign."

He chuckled. "I hate to admit it, but..." He chuckled again.

Having nothing to do and quite lonely in his quiet

apartment one evening, he had been walking around Kokusai when he came across the English sign. It was a relief to come across something he could read. Especially when it mentioned Okinawan pigs feet soup. He had gone upstairs into the tiny restaurant and ordered a bowl of their soup. Something he had not had for ages. Ever since Grandma died.

Now, climbing up the steep stairway, not feeling lonely with Reiko besides him, he momentarily forgot about the e-mail and looked forward to having a big bowl of soup.

As they turned into the doorway, a couple was about to leave.

"Chris," the man said, "what are you doing here?"

It was Professor Akira Nakada from Ryudai's English Department. He first met Akira at UH when Akira was a graduate student there.

"You like their soup, too?" Chris asked.

"The best soup in all Okinawa," said Akira, and introduced his wife.

Chris was about to introduce Reiko. Akira, however, immediately recognized her. "Kinjo-san," he said, "you're acting as Professor Yamashiro's guide?"

"She's a very good guide," said Chris, before Reiko could reply. "She took me all over southern Okinawa today."

"That's very nice of you, Kinjo-san," Akira said.

"It was fun," said Reiko.

"Well, we'll see you at school," said Akira. "The soup is especially good tonight," he added. "Good night."

"Good night," said Chris and Reiko.

Chris caught Reiko a little concerned. "You took classes from him?"

Reiko nodded. "I hope he doesn't think it's not proper for me to be seen with you here."

"Not proper?"

"I'm a student; you're a professor."

"So?"

"The university frowns on professors and students getting too... You know..."

"Too close?"

Reiko nodded, stepping over to the closest table.

"You took me around to see Okinawa," he said, following Reiko, sitting across from her at the table. "I'm sure Akira won't put more into it than that."

"I hope not."

The mid-forties waitress approached their table graciously. Recognizing Chris, she said, "Ah so... Mata kimashita, neh. Domo arigato gozai masu."

"She said thank you for returning," Reiko interpreted.

Chris, understanding that much Japanese, bowed, and said, "Arigato... I'm glad to be back."

Reiko translated and the waitress bowed gratefully.

"We, both of us, want your soup," said Chris.

Reiko translated.

"Hai," the lady said, bowing again, then stepped into the kitchen.

"How did you order when you first came here?" Reiko asked.

"I pointed to that picture up there," he said, indicating a photo of a bowl of soup. "And I said, 'Onegai shimasu.'"

"That's pretty good."

"Like back home, two magic words: 'Please and thank you.'"

After a rather long break in their conversation and still waiting for their soup, Reiko, apparently very curious asked, "That e-mail, was it from your wife?"

He looked at her. "No," he said, "Not from her, about her."

"Oh."

"You heard me, huh?"

She nodded.

"We're getting a divorce," he said, bitterly.

"Oh?"

"One of the reasons I took the position here," he said. "To get away from her and hopefully…"

"Things would work out?

He shook his head. "Too late for that."

Reiko said nothing.

"I just hope Carrie, our daughter, won't take it too hard."

Reiko remained silent.

"It's always hardest on the child," he said.

Reiko nodded.

"I heard divorce rates are pretty high here in Japan, too."

"It is getting that way."

"Back home, it's one out of every two marriages."

"That much?"

"In some places, even worse."

"Worse than fifty percent?"

Chris nodded. Grimly.

"Makes you wonder why people bother to get married," he said.

"Like all young couples we thought we had a perfect marriage going. You know... Security, social position, goals, a child...

"You never know," he added, "you just never know..."

"The latest government survey show that Okinawa has the highest divorce rate in Japan," Reiko said.

"The highest?" Chris said, shocked.

Reiko nodded.

"All the couples I see seem to be very happy."

"Yes," Reiko said. "Seem to be very happy." Then added, "Divorces still have their stigma."

"So they stick it out?"

"For their children's sake."

"Your liberal abortion law in Japan," he said. "Isn't that what keeps families from having unwanted children?"

"Children are not unwanted during the early days of a marriage," she said.

"Except for the first child," he said. "You know, the first child is almost always born prematurely."

Chris could not hold back laughter.

The waitress at last brought their soup.

She apologized. "Sumimasen. Watashi dake shigoto shite imasu."

"She's the only one working here tonight," Reiko explained.

"Hai, wakari masu," Chris said." Yes, I understand.

"Nihongo yoku wakarimasu, neh?" the waitress said to

Chris. You understand Japanese very well.

"Hai, sukoshi hanashimasu," said Chris. Yes. I speak a little Japanese.

The waitress placed the tray of steaming bowls on the table, served Chris first, then Reiko.

The mouth-watering aroma of the pigs feet soup made Chris salivate. Protruding out of the bowl were huge slices of pinkish pig's feet cut at the ankles. In the soup were exotic Okinawan spices with cuts of onions, cabbage, potato and some other kind of vegetables that he had never tasted before.

They were given only chopsticks and it was hard to pick up the pig's feet with them. After a moment, he noticed Reiko going through the ritual of bringing the hot bowl up to her lips and drinking the soup.

Why not? he said to himself, and began slurping the soup.

"Ah, Okinawan soup..." he finally said, placing his chopsticks down into the empty bowl, wiping his mouth, "it sure brings back fond memories of grandma."

"Has she been gone a long time?" Reiko asked, also placing her chopsticks in the bowl.

"When Carrie was just six years old," he said. "She still misses her great grandma."

"She liked her great-grandma's Okinawan dishes?"

"Loved every one of them."

"Her mother, too?"

"Rose? She hated Okinawan food."

"She's not an Okinawan?"

"Hiroshima. Actually she wasn't against Okinawans.

Her parents were. Thought they were way above us. And they were cane field laborers like everyone else!"

"It was one of the problems about your marriage?"

"She being Hiroshima; me Okinawan? Nah," he said. "Nothing like that. Our problem was far more personal."

"Oh?"

"You don't want to know about it," he said.

Chapter 11:
Ishikawa POW Camp

After walking back to Chris' apartment, she drove home to Nishihara, still thinking what a day it had been. Of course, it was a shock to discover that Chris and his wife were about to get a divorce. She had thought they were an ideal couple. The Yuta was right. If they were a happy couple Chris would have brought his wife to Okinawa with him.

She had thought Chris would eventually invite his wife to Okinawa. The Yuta, on the other hand, saw what Chris was going through the moment she met him. How could you not believe in the powers of a Yuta?

She suddenly thought of meeting Professor Nakada at the restaurant. Like Chris said, he's not going to put more into her and Chris being there together. Goodness! She hoped not. If a rumor started that she and Chris were more than, well...a student/professor friends, Chris would be called into the Chairman's office.

She remembered all too well the scandal of Professor Matayoshi and one of his history students meeting each other at hotels. The Dean had called Professor Matayoshi into his office and warned him if the relationship continued he, the Dean, would have to ask the professor to submit a resignation. The girl had claimed that the professor promised to marry her as soon as he obtained a divorce from his wife. Which the professor denied he had said. The professor, nevertheless, resigned from Ryudai and moved on to a university in the Mainland.

It was quite late when she parked her car in the driveway. There was no light in the living room nor in the bedroom of her father and mother.

She opened the front door quietly and slipped into her bedroom. Still alert, her mind still churning with the day's events; she knew she wouldn't be able to fall asleep. How could she? Not after learning about poor Chris. He and his wife had been married for over 23 years. And now a divorce! "You never know…" like Chris said.

Oh, Reiko! she chided herself. It's none of your business. He's just one of fifty percent of Americans who go through divorces.

No school tomorrow, she decided to work on Ojii-chan's Chronicle. She had translated quite a few pages so far. If she kept it up she could translate the whole Chronicle in a month or so. She was sure Chris would be surprised when she showed it to him. She had thought of showing him parts of it as she went along, then decided not to. The Chronicle led to an unexpected ending. The beginning and the middle would not make sense without discovering what really happened to Ojii-chan at the end.

In a few minutes, she was at her desk, her Japanese/English dictionary beside her.

She pictured Ojii-chan sitting there before her, instructing her to use the right English words and phrases in the translation.

Rei-chan, since you have come this far, you must surely know how happy I am having you do the translation. Please continue as though it is your own writings.

Franky, my former enemy and now my friend, was about to leave Ishikawa POW Camp any day to join the American offense at Shuri Castle. They need more soldiers like him to help the wounded.

My English has improved very much since I am able to practice it with Franky. He is a kind man. His father and mother and his sisters and brothers back home in America must be like him.

One day, he brought me a magazine he just received from home. It had a big picture of a middle-aged man with a cigarette in his mouth and a helmet on his head. He was not a soldier, but a civilian who was with the soldiers at war. Franky explained that the man was Ernie Pyle who was killed in Ie Jimu a month ago.

The man seemed to have warm, kind eyes, not the eyes of hatred or revenge, but of deep understanding and compassion. He was in the frontlines because he wanted to share the dangers the young GIs were going through and to write to Americans back home about the horrors of wars. I read the magazine and began sharing the man's feelings. Wars, he said, are not glamorous or glorious. They are full of miseries, fears and sufferings.

It was about this time that Franky told me if he survived the war, he would return home and prepare himself to do some good in his life. He showed me a photo of a young high school girl he planned to marry. His girlfriend would become a nurse and he would become a doctor. Who knows, he said, maybe someday I'll come back to Okinawa and see what Okinawa is really like *without all the fighting and destructions going on. He said he would also like to meet Okinawan people in time of peace and not see so much hate, fear and mistrust in their eyes.*

Ojii-chan, she prayed, your Franky did come back to Okinawa. I met him at Ernie-san's park. Franky is now Dr. Frank Sweeney. His wife, Annie, is the high school girlfriend he said he was going to marry. She became a nurse.

Your Franky remembered you, Ojii-chan. One of the reasons he returned to Okinawa was to see his friend, "Kenny." And find out what had happened to you after the war. He was awfully sorry that he did not come back a few months earlier when you were still with us.

She went back and read the last entry again. She had, of course, heard about the battles of Okinawa, but had not thought of Uchinanchus showing hate, fear and mistrust for the Americans. They hid and ran away from the Americans because the Japanese soldiers had told them that the barbaric Americans would kill every man, woman and child on the island. Also that they would rape every girl, young and old, before beheading them.

She went on with the translation.

My companions in our concrete machine gun pillbox were ready and willing to die for our Emperor. So was I. I lost one of my legs; they lost their lives. I did not die because I was unconscious when the Americans charged into our pillbox and found me bleeding to death. They could have left me there and gone on with their battle. But they stopped the bleeding, gave me something to stop the terrible pain, then transported me out of Ie Jima and brought me to our POW camp. Who would have thought Americans would save my life minutes after they had tried to kill me?

When soldiers talk about enemies, the enemies are collectively thought of as less than human beings. When you meet them in person, they become fellow human beings with the same values and same goals as your own.

My prayers are for Franky to survive the rest of the battle in Okinawa and return home safely. He is here not to kill, but to save lives.

He reminded me of an American Christian missionary who came to Ie Jima long before the war and told us about Christianity. It was a foreign religion for all of us and we were not interested in anything but our own religion of ancestral worship. I wish I had learned more about Christianity. Meeting Franky, who is a dedicated Christian, had made me believe that there is more to life than ancestral worship. It is worshipping a Kami-sama, a god, who is kind, caring and just. It is a Kami-sama who teaches goodness, kindness and forgiveness.

Meeting Franky made me search for the truth of his religion by his example. I hope I will continue to search for the truth of his beliefs and also be an example of those beliefs.

This war, this horrible war, is only teaching us more hatred. It is the same as placing a criminal in jail to change him; only to have him come out of jail even worse than he had been because he learned more hatred in jail. We Japanese soldiers were taught to hate Americans. That Americans were uncivilized, cannibals, inhuman. And I'm sure that's what the Americans were taught about us. Maybe, some good will come out of this war. We will finally meet each other and discover that we have more in common than not. That we all have families, neighbors, friends and loved ones. That given a chance we can learn to know each other and get along as brothers.

Oh, Rei-chan, there are so much I'd like to share with you, you who have your whole life ahead of you, you who can become not only a teacher at a university, but a teacher for everyone. There are so much goodness to spread in this world; goodness that will get people together, goodness that will make loved ones out of strangers and enemies.

There was a time when I wished I had died in that pillbox. To have killed an American and die a brave death for the Emperor. When I discovered that I had only one leg left, I prayed that I would die. Had the Americans left me in that pillbox, I surely would have reached for the hand grenade and blown myself up. Was it fate that the Americans found me before I could do that? That the Americans who found me were kind and forgiving? My only concern at that time was, did I kill an American? Did I fulfill my duty?

Reiko wiped her eyes. Oh, Ojii-chan.

She took a long breath. She wiped her eyes again. She wished the Chronicle ended there.

She continued on.

Franky not only became a friend of mine, he became friends of other POWs. And, they, like myself, changed their attitude toward Americans. Actually, Franky was supposed to be treating only the wounded Americans in a nearby American military hospital, but because he had helped us and got to know us when we were first brought into the POW hospital, he kept coming back. At first, the other American medic-guards resented Franky for being too friendly with us. They eventually accepted Franky for what he was.

Franky was still in Ishikawa when the Americans started to invade Shuri Castle. From what we heard, the battle went on for days. The Americans advanced, then had to retreat when reinforcement for the Japanese soldiers kept coming back. We, of course, knew that our soldiers would never surrender. That they would fight to the very end.

If they only knew, I thought. If they only knew that they would be treated well as POWs.

We were always glad to see Franky in the mornings, knowing he was still at our POW camp and not where all the battles were taking place.

One day, he came to see me with a GI shoe. Also with a pair of crutches. The shoe was for my left foot. My right foot was, of course, gone. Both the crutches and the shoe had belonged to a wounded GI who was transferred to an American hospital ship. The GI must have been big and tall. The crutches had to be shortened and the shoe filled with newspapers.

I was now able to walk with the crutches and a shoe instead of a slipper. I did not have to thank Franky. He saw the tears of gratefulness in my eyes and knew how much the crutches and the shoe meant to me.

The shoe and crutches have been replaced today, but they will always be a part of my life. They are the ones that are in the corner of our living room. Close to our obutsudan altar.

When Obaa-chan and families of us POWs found out we were in a camp in Ishikawa, they started arriving there day after day. They could not enter the POW camp, but were allowed to stand outside the fence and talk to us. Many, including Obaa-chan, brought food that we craved, fried fish, pickled vegetable, Okinawan sweet potatoes, sometimes rice and boiled pork in delicious gravy.

The guards at first were suspicious. They were afraid we would be getting weapons. But soon discovered the furoshiki wrappings contained only Okinawan food. Some of the guards tasted the food just to make sure they are just food. And they seemed to enjoy them.

There were still fanatical POWs from Mainland Japan. They sang Japanese military songs and marched around the camp. Most of us Uchinanchu POWs did not join them. The guards let them do whatever they wanted to do, just as long as they did not try to escape or start a riot. Some even went on hunger strikes. When they saw us Uchinanchus enjoying the food that our families brought to the fence, they envied us. Before long, they said they won't eat American POW food, but were willing to eat our Uchinanchu food, which we shared with them.

The Japanese military songs and the marching soon stopped. Some of them began eating American POW food like the rest of us: pork and beans, mashed potatoes, hot dogs and hard biscuits.

We kept hearing that Ushijima Taisho was winning the Shuri Castle battle and was pushing the Americans back to the sea. If that was so, why were so many American ships still landing more troops? We also heard that the kamikaze airplanes were sinking most of the American ships. If that was so, how come there are still hundreds of American ships in the bay?

Of course, we all wanted the Japanese troops to win the battle of Okinawa. But we knew about the superiority of the American troops and the powerful weapons they had. Ie Jima itself was supposed to have been invincible. It took the Americans just a few days to conquer it.

Kawaiso na, I said to myself. It is a pity that so many would *have to die. There were at least 100,000 Japanese troops on Okinawa. Will they all have to die before realizing how foolish it is to keep on fighting? I did not share my thoughts with my fellow POWs. I was still a Japanese soldier.*

Chapter 12: Yogi Park

The news and the TV programs at the apartment were all in Japanese. Which he could barely understand. He could, however, understand the baseball games. Baseball was "basu-ball-u", a homerun, "hom-u run-u" a strike, "stri-ku."

It was the news that were most frustrating. He looked at the pictures, but had to guess what the announcer was saying. Some of the news was about America, and he wanted to know what it was all about, but could only infer and guess from the pictures.

Then he discovered that the prefectural library, about a mile away in Yogi Park, had the Japan Times which was in English. He began walking to the library, a good exercise, and started reading the Japan Times. What he really wanted to do was to check the business section and see how the New York Stock Exchange was doing. To his relief the mutual funds belonging to him and Rose were the same as when he left home.

While browsing through the library one day, he discovered a section of English books. He had read most of them back home until he came across books which were about the Okinawan battles and famous men involved in the battles. Prominent among them was a book about Ernie Pyle, the war correspondent who was killed on Ie Jima.

The same island that Reiko had mentioned, her island.

He removed the book from the shelf and sat at the reading table. It was a book called "Ernie Pyle's War," by James Tobin. In the book jacket the York Times Book Review said, *This is the portrait of a complex, enormously gifted but tortured writer...but it is much more: few books about combat journalism have so vividly depicted the fascinating interactions between war correspondents, soldiers and folks back home... World War II was quintessentially Ernie Pyle's war, and Mr. Tobin brilliantly explains why.*

Chris had heard about Ernie Pyle, but all he really about knew him was that he was buried at the National Memorial Cemetery of the Pacific in Punchbowl, Honolulu.

Before reading the book he checked other endorsements and appraisals of the book. The Publishers Weekly said that *Ernie Pyle, better than any other World War II journalist, conveyed triumphs and tribulations of the common soldier trying to survive a brutal conflict. From North Africa and Normandy, Anzio and Okinawa—where he died—Pyle brought the war home to America. James Tobin's superbly documented and compassionate account.*

It was odd that he had not known anything about the book nor other books written about Ernie Pyle. Perhaps, it was because the war correspondents in World War II did not interest him.

He wanted to borrow book but couldn't. He had no prefectural library card. To obtain one might take days. What he could do was to order whatever books there were about Ernie Pyle from "Amazon.Com."

He now thumbed through Tobin's book, reading more

thoroughly parts that were intensely interesting about Ernie Pyle. Pyle was in his mid-forties when he landed in North Africa, Normandy, and Okinawa. He was already a famous correspondent in the States and had volunteered to serve as an overseas war correspondent. He landed with the troops in the midst of battles and narrowly escaped death several times.

He became the famous war correspondent whose articles were read by millions of Americans back home. He told Americans of the horrors of war and how the GIs were fighting with courage and bravery for their country. His columns were more about the low-ranking soldiers than the generals and admirals. For this he was revered by all working-class Americans who had sons, husbands and brothers fighting overseas. He was a friend of all the GIs and became a hero of theirs. He was looked up to by military leaders who knew that his columns were morale boosters for the common GI. He even became a guest of the President at the White House when he returned home for well-deserved breaks from the front lines.

Having gone through most of the book which took place primarily in Europe, Chris kept wondering what made Ernie Pyle come to the Pacific. He had accomplished what most war correspondents could ever accomplish or experience in a lifetime, yet was willing to keep risking his life. He had expressed to his fellow correspondents on several occasions how lucky he had been in the front and wondered how long his luck would hold up.

He landed on several tiny Pacific islands with the Marines and GIs, and wrote about the Pacific battle fronts.

On April 1, 1945, during the invasion of Okinawa, he landed on the island and spent several uneventful days there. He then returned to the command ship and prepared for another landing. This time on Ie Jima, a tiny ten-square-mile island near the western coast of Okinawa.

Author James Tobin said that before the landing Ernie Pyle wrote to a friend: *I've got almost a spooky feeling that I've been spared once more and that I would be asking for it to tempt fate again. So I'm going to keep my promise to you and to myself that that was the last one. I'll be on operations in the future, of course, but not on any more landings.*

He landed on Ie Jima on April 17 and interviewed several infantry men. After spending the night near the beach, he ate his cold C rations in the morning, then hitched a ride on a jeep with a Colonel Joseph Coolidge who was heading for a new regimental post.

James Tobin wrote: *The fighting was inland, so the road from the beach was quiet. At about ten o'clock, a Japanese Nambu machine gun chattered. Pyle, Coolidge and the other men in the jeep leaped out and jumped into a ditch along the road. After a moment Ernie raised his head and the machine gunner fired again, hitting him in the left temple just below the line of the helmet.*

Chris shook his head. After all the landings and battlefields he had gone through which were far more fierce and dangerous than in Ie Jima, Ernie Pyle had to be killed by an insignificant Japanese soldier hiding in the bushes with a machine gun.

Returning the book to the shelf, he decided to order the same book from Amazon.Com, plus other books Amazon might have on Ernie Pyle. They could be helpful for Reiko's translation.

Besides, he'd like to go through the book thoroughly and not thumb through it like he just did. Ernie Pyle, according to Tobin, was a great American writer. A writer who cared about the common man and wrote about the common man that he knew so well. Chris felt that had Ernie Pyle lived through the war, he would have written a great story about GIs like those James Jones had written in From Here To Eternity.

Stepping out of the library, he wondered if Reiko's Ojii-chan's Chronicle mentions the death of Ernie Pyle. Ojii-chan, of course, could not have met Ernie Pyle. As far as he knew, Ojii-chan was a wounded POW in Ishikawa when Ernie Pyle landed with the Marines.

Outside, he sat at the concrete bench and watched the pigeons and tiny birds fighting for the scattered bread crumbs and cookies on the walkway. When a dog came by the pigeons and birds would fly away and return as soon as the dog went away.

Across the way, sitting on goza mats spread over the green grass, were several middle-aged men and women drinking sake or beer listening to a man strumming on his sanshin and singing old traditional Okinawan songs. When the music turned to a lively tune and the singer sang with gusto, one of the women jumped up from the goza mat and danced joyfully. The others began clapping in time with the music and joined in the singing. In a second, another woman jumped up and joined the first woman, both laughing and enjoying themselves.

Uchinanchus, Chris said to himself, just like the native Hawaiians back home. Strum a ukulele and someone would start singing and dancing the hula. Island people. They're all the same everywhere. Happy, uninhibited, aways laughing, singing...

When the sanshin player changed into a more subdued number, the two women sat down and listened solemnly. And so did Chris. It brought back memories of the old Kailua days when Grandpa, Grandma and the Okinawan neighbors would get together and reminisce over their younger days back home. Grandpa, who was once a sanshin teacher, would start plucking on his sanshin and sing old village songs. Like the sanshin player on the gaza mat was doing now.

One of the songs Chris remembered was about a young man who is engaged to a lovely young girl and is about to sail off from Naha Harbor to Brazil. He promises the young girl that he would return home soon with lots of money and they would get married and live happily ever after. In the second verse, the young man writes to his bride-to-be from Brazil and expresses regret that he had come to Brazil without her. In the third verse, the young man now in his fifth year in Brazil, begs forgiveness from his bride-to-be. He confesses that in his loneliness he started to live with a Portuguese woman who is the mother of two children and is expecting a third one which is his. "Please forgive me... Please forgive me..." the refrain goes on. "Please forget me... Please forget me..." it ends begging his bride-to-be to go on with her own life.

Chris remembers Grandma telling him that the words

to the song were actually written by a young Okinawan man who married a Portuguese girl and made Brazil his home. As for the girl back in Okinawa, she, too, became a mother after marrying an Okinawan man.

A sad story with a not-too-sad ending, Grandma had said.

The sunshin player across the way now started another song and began singing a soft plaintiff refrain that subdued the crowd around him. Although not understanding the words, Chris could remember that night many years ago when he was staying with Grandpa and Grandma while his father and mother went to Honolulu.

Uncle Shinyei who lived with Grandpa and Grandma had not yet returned to the kitchen table after taking a hot furo bath.

Uncle Shinyei had arrived from Okinawa several years ago, and was working at Grandpa's farm. He was hoping to save enough money to return to his wife and daughter in Okinawa, and build a home in Ginoza Village.

Grandpa had again read a letter that had arrived that day. He and Grandma had not yet shared the news with Uncle Shinyei.

When Uncle finally stepped into the kitchen and sat at the table to have his dinner, Grandpa took out the letter from the envelope.

"This came today," he said softly and handed the letter to Uncle.

Uncle, a younger brother of Grandpa, looked at the letter in Grandpa's hand.

"For me?" he asked, reaching.

"I guess our onisan *older brother* in Okinawa thought it would be better if I told you," Grandpa said.

Uncle looked at the letter, hesitating.

When he finally read the letter, his head went down and he said nothing.

"There's nothing you can do about it now," Grandpa said, looking at Uncle, then across the table at Grandma who was now wiping her eyes.

Uncle sat there silently, his head down, his eyes brimming with tears.

"It must have been very hard for your wife to keep waiting for you," Grandma said sadly to Uncle.

"Maybe you shouldn't have stayed this long," Grandpa said.

Chris listening, but no quite comprehending all that was being said, looked at his uncle. He knew there was sadness in what was being said and he shared Uncle's pain.

"Do you wish to go back?" Grandpa said.

Uncle thought it over for a second. Finally, he said, "As long as Kimi-chan is alright with her auntie, I'd like to stay a little longer."

Instead of having his dinner, Uncle rose with the letter in his hand, and went into his bedroom adjoining the kitchen.

While Grandpa and Grandma sat silently at the kitchen table, and Chris held Grandma's hand, Uncle began playing his sanshin and singing softly. Like the man across the way Uncle kept singing and playing his sanshin forlornly, lonelily, his voice reaching out to all corners of the world.

Chris would learn later that Uncle's wife had gone to the Philippines with a man from the next village, and would never return to Okinawa.

Thinking of that night when Dad and Mom went to Honolulu and left him with Grandpa and Grandma, Chris realized that he had not heard from Douglas in Honolulu for over a week. Has he convinced Rose that the Kailua property was not to be negotiated? That it had nothing to do with their divorce. He hoped Douglas would be tough and tell Rose that if she continued to play hard ball he, Chris, would have no choice but to settle in court. Which meant disclosing the photos he had of her leaving the hotel room with her haole boss.

Chapter 13: Rumor

While Chris was walking back to his apartment from Yogi Park, Reiko was in her bedroom translating another chapter of Ojii-chan's Chronicle.

The translations were now more than half finished and she had printed them. She was building up the Chronicle for the suspenseful ending and was eager to come to it.

Reiko resumed translating.

It was over a month since I became a POW at Ishikawa and my missing right leg was not missed as much as when I first lost it. I was now able to use the crutches Franky had given me as though it was a part of my body. The oversized shoe on my left foot was now filled with rags and they were much more comfortable than newspapers.

Franky was no longer with us. His outfit was transferred to the South where the battles were getting more fierce each day. I had hoped to say goodbye to Franky before he left and wish him a safe journey, but he had left at sunrise and the POW camp was not the same anymore. Fresh guards and new medical personnel had taken over, and they were not as friendly and caring as Franky's outfit.

Our families continued bringing food and speaking to us through the fence whenever the new guards allowed them. They told us that the battle of Shuri Castle was still going on and that

Ushijima Taisho and his staff were still there fighting the Americans bravely. The castle was so well fortified with its thick concrete walls that the Americans were unable to penetrate the walls and enter the castle grounds. It was only when the big ships in the bay fired their powerful guns at the castle and destroyed it that the American ground troops finally marched in. By that time, most of the surviving Japanese troops were marching toward the South where they intended to fight to the last man.

I, of course, hoped that Franky would be fine and would soon be able to return home. He, after all, was not a soldier trying to kill his enemies; he was a soldier who is trying to save the lives of his enemies as well as his fellow American soldiers. Someday, maybe, we will meet again. In another place, another time, and under other more favorable conditions.

I had given Franky the cat I whittled from a tree branch. I hoped he would be able to take it home as a souvenir and remember that there was an "enemy soldier" he had met who considered him a friend. Yes, that would be wonderful. Out of the ashes of a terrible war emerged an ever-lasting friendship. I will keep praying for Franky's safe return home to that place called Indiana.

To get over the boredom of life in a POW camp, I made a sanshin from metal cans I found in the camp dumps. I smoothed the cans, shaped them into the head of a sanshin, and attached whatever wires I could find. The music that came out of it was not as musical as the regular sanshin, but it provided us with an instrument that made us want to sing and forget the battles that were going on.

Our families told us through the fence horrible accounts of

Uchinanchu families caught in the crossfire between Americans and Japanese soldiers, and thousands of them had been killed. There were stories of Japanese soldiers killing Uchinanchus for food and water in the caves. Also of killing babies in the caves to keep them from crying and revealing their hideout. In the South, near Mabuni, where the last battles were taking place, the families heard of young high school nurse volunteers dying with the Japanese soldiers rather than surrendering.

Wartime hysteria and rumors were everywhere. Somehow, our families heard that American airplanes were bombing Tokyo, Yokohama, Kobe and other major cities in Japan as they did Naha. How long will the war keep going on? Until everyone was killed? Until there were no Japanese left? Why aren't they negotiating for peace and stop all the killings?

Reiko could now hear the telephone ringing in the living room and Dad or Mom answering it.

In a second, her dad called out in English, "Reiko! It's for you!"

Rising from her desk, she went out of her bedroom and stepped into the living room. Dad had placed the telephone on the coffee table and was watching the U.S. Air Force TV station.

"Moshi moshi..."

"It's me, Chris," said the reply.

"Chris?"

"I've found a place where they serve American food," Chris went on. "Steak and French fries. Wanna go?"

"Now?" she said. "Tonight?" "If you're busy; some other time."

"I just started another chapter of Ojii-chan's memorir,

but I guess it can wait," she said.

"The restaurant is the American Seamen's Club near the harbor," he said. "Know where it is?"

"The Seamen's Club? I've been there with my dad and mom several times. Dad's a member there."

"So, okay?" he said. "In about half-an-hour?"

"Yes. I'll be over in half-an-hour."

Hanging up, she turned to her dad, "Do they let anyone in at the Seamen's Club now?"

"You still need a membership card," he said.

"I wonder if he knows that."

"Who?"

"Professor Yamashiro."

"I think they'll let him if he has an American passport," said Dad.

"He must have heard about it," she said.

Dad said nothing for a moment. Then, "You're seeing a lot of him, aren't you?"

"Professor Yamashiro?"

"What happened to that boy you used to go out with before you went to UH?"

"Taichi? Taichi Shimabukuro?"

"Seemed like a nice boy."

"Yeah, he is. A nice boy."

"That professor, isn't he about my age?"

"Oh, Dad. We're just good friends. And he's going to help me with Ojii-chan's translation. Maybe even help me get it published."

"That translation, you coming along okay?"

"I can't wait to show it to you, Dad."

"Grandma asked Mom about it the other day. Don't keep her waiting too long."

"I'll go over the Japanese version with her as soon as I'm done with the English version."

"You've got everyone wondering what it's all about."

"All of us, Dad, we thought we knew Ojii-chan."

"We didn't?"

Reiko shook her head. "He kept many things to himself."

"Like?"

"Dad! I have to be going. Chris is expecting me."

"He's not Professor Yamashiro anymore?"

They exchanged looks for a moment. She then went back into her bedroom to change and to put on a little makeup.

She was at Chris' apartment in forty-five minutes, the early-evening commuting traffic bad as usual.

Chris was waiting at the sidewalk in the front of the apartment's office. He hopped into the Toyota and saved Reiko the trouble of parking.

She drove toward Naha Harbor, going through side streets and avoiding the heavy traffic whenever possible. They were at American Seamen's Club shortly. The parking lot was not yet full, but quite a few American as well as Okinawan patrons were already at the front door waiting for it to open.

After parking, she and Chris joined the patrons at the doorway showing their membership cards. Chris took out his American passport, showed it to the Okinawan hostess who looked at it, up at Chris, then smiling, welcomed him and Reiko in.

Unlike the small and narrow Okinawan restaurants, the Seamen's Club had a spacious dining room, a bar, a pool room and a huge kitchen in the back. The aroma was not fried tempura or sukiyaki, but steaks and hamburgers.

The Filipino waiter, who spoke English quite well, was taking their orders in a few minutes. Chris ordered the biggest ribeye steak they had, medium done, with lots of French fries, green salad and a glass of American Budweiser beer. Except for the beer, Reiko ordered the same thing.

"How did you find out about this place?" Reiko asked.

"The office girl at the apartment," he replied. "When I asked if there was an American restaurant in Naha, she mentioned this place. All I needed is an American passport."

"More and more Uchinanchus are becoming members here," said Reiko. "They miss the American food they used to have when living in the States."

"I love Japanese and Okinawan food, but I needed a change. Good old steak and French fries."

"And good old American beer, huh?"

"If they had good old Hawaiian Primo I would've ordered it," he said.

Reiko suddenly noticed Chris looking toward the door.
She turned. It was Professor Miyazato and his wife.
Chris quickly rose. "Well, look who's here?" he greeted.
"Hi, Chris," Professor Miyazato returned.
Reiko quickly rose, too. "Hi, Sensei" she said, bowing deeply, "Hello, Okusan" she said to his wife, recognizing her courteously.

Mrs. Miyazato bowed back. "How are you, Kinjo-san?" she said, then bowed to Chris.

The formalities over, Chris invited the Miyazatos to join them. Professor Miyazato, however, declined. He and his wife will be waiting for faculty friends to join them.

"Kinjo-san," said Professor Miyazato, "I understand you've been very busy translating your grandfather's Chronicle."

"Hai, Sensei. It's taking up most of my time."

"If you don't mind, I'd like to read it when you're done."

"I'll be very glad to show it to you, Sensei."

"We'll see if it can qualify as your thesis for your graduate studies."

"Domo arigato gozaimasu," *Thank you very much.* Reiko bowed deeply.

Professor Miyazato now turned to Chris.

"Made up your mind, Chris?"

"Not yet, Takashi. I'm still waiting for advice from my lawyer."

"Well, let me know," Professor Miyazato said. "The Chairman will have to find a substitute while you're gone."

"I'll let you know in a couple of days."

"No hurry. Think about it very carefully."

"I will," said Chris.

"Well, I see our guest coming in," said Professor Miyazato, turning toward the door, waving to a couple stepping in. "Drop by the office anytime," he said to Chris, stepping away. "That goes for you too, Kinjo-san. If there's anything I can do to help you with the translation let me know."

"Domo arigato, Sensei," said Reiko, bowing.

Professor Miyazato and his wife left to join their guest a few tables away. Okinawan men were getting Americanized, she thought. Professor Miyazato had brought his wife to dinner and so did his friend. Normally, Okinawan husbands left their wives home when they met other men at restaurants.

"You're going back?" she asked, when the Miyazatos were beyond hearing range.

Chris nodded.

"For good?"

"Just for a few days. My divorce."

"She won't give it to you?"

"Yeah, she will. After taking what doesn't belong to her."

"Oh?"

"Don't ever get a divorce," he said.

"Divorce? Me?"

"When you get married."

"Think of a divorce when I get married?"

The waiter brought their order, the huge steak sizzling on the plates, the French fries steaming hot, the tiny squared butters melting beside the biscuits.

"Enjoy," said the waiter. "Please let me know if you want anything else."

"Right," said Chris, picking up his knife and fork and slicing off a chunk of his steak.

The juicy, nose-tingling aroma of the medium-done steak and the French fries suddenly took Reiko back to

Manoa Valley near the UH campus where she used to treat herself to steak and French fries whenever she could afford them.

"Never thought I'd ever miss American food," said Chris, chewing quite fast, digging into his French fries, sipping his Budweiser.

It was wonderful to see Chris enjoying himself so much. In a few more minutes, he called the waiter and ordered another Budweiswer.

"You've never tasted beer?" he asked her.

Reiko nodded. "Once. I didn't like the smell."

"Sake?"

"Once, too. It was worse than beer."

"Unusual these days when women don't drink."

"Your wife, she drinks?"

"Sometimes, too much."

"To keep up with you?"

"I usually stop after a couple of beers."

She kept on eating, sorry she had brought up his wife.

She glanced over at Professor Miyazato's table. Their guests were the Vice-President of Ryudai and his wife, a professor of German at the university.

She wondered if Professor Miyazato would put more into her and Chris having dinner together at the Seamen's Club. Why would he? He knows Chris will be helping her with the Chronicle and that they have become good friends. Especially since she's been Chris' chauffeur on several occasions.

"If I have to leave," Chris now said between bites, "will you take over the class?

"Me?"

"It'll just be for a couple of classes."

"What am I supposed to do?"

"I'll assign some of the students chapters to read. Then, you'll conduct discussions on their readings."

"No grades?" she asked.

"No grades," he said. "Just discussions. Keep the class busy. When I'm back we'll talk about the chapters."

"Professor Miyazato and the Chairman of the department know?"

"Not yet. But I'm sure they'll go along. They know of your academic achievements. Besides, the discussion will be about Hawaii.

"It'll be a good experience for you," he went on. "A handle on how to lecture a literature class."

"Well..." said Reiko. "If you really think I can handle it..."

"No problem."

A moment of silence.

Then, "If your wife won't give you a divorce..."

"She will," he said. "She's got no choice."

"No choice?"

"Not a pleasant subject," he said, taking another sip of his beer. "Divorces," he added, shaking his head. "Ever heard of a pleasant divorce?"

She looked at him, now sorry she had brought up the subject.

Chris took another sip. "Look," he said, "about the class while I'm gone. The important thing is keep everyone occupied. Have everyone involved in the discussions."

"I'll try," she said.

"I know you will," he said.

She pictured herself taking over Chris' class. All the students the same age as herself. Will they resent her? Demand to know what she'll tell Chris about their conduct?

On the other hand, as Chris said, it will be a good experience. It might lead to other assignments. And someday, who knows? It might lead to a temporary teaching position while she's doing her graduate studies. Then, eventually a full-time position when she receives her Ph.D.

Finally finished with their dinner, Chris ordered apple pie for dessert. And American coffee.

"You think Professor Miyazato might think there's more to our teacher/student relationship?" she asked, once more glancing toward Professor Miyazato's table.

"Nah, "said Chris, "he knows there's nothing going on between us."

"I hope so."

"You hope there was?" Chris said, and laughed.

"Oh, Chris..."

"He knows I'm old enough to be your grandfather," he said.

"Grandfather?"

"Father."

"That's bad?"

"Not good."

The waiter brought their dessert.

"That boy I saw you talking to in the hallway the other

day," he said, taking a bite of his apple pie, "he seemed interested in you."

"We used to go out once," she said, slicing a piece of her pie with her fork, "before I went to UH."

"Not anymore?"

She shook her head. "We're just good friends now."

"Ah, to be young again…" he said, chuckling.

"Oh, Chris, you're not that old…"

Chapter 14:
The Photos

There was an e-mail from Honolulu.

Didn't want to, but she left me no choice, Douglas started. *Showed her the pictures you gave me. And got tough as you suggested. Rose being Rose, she denied everything. Fake pictures, she claimed. And started yelling at me. At you, too. All the way to Okinawa?*

You and me, we're sonsfabitches! Bastards! Perverts!! She'll sue you for invasion of privacy. You know where she got that? She's apparently never heard of 'Truth is a defense.'

I told her to have her new attorney call me. We'll either settle or go to court. This morning, her attorney, Rich Littleton, an acquaintance, called. We'll be getting together in a few days. From Rich's tone, she's ready to settle. The only settlement, I told him, is that the farmland is all yours. And the rest of the assets be divided as originally discussed. Okay?

Chris threw his hands up and clapped! A monkey off his back! Not really a slam-dunk. But just as great. Just as satisfying. He really wouldn't have let Douglas use the pictures in the courtroom.

He couldn't. He just didn't have the stomach to let Carrie know that her mother is a... A goddamn whore. Which, in a way, Rose is. She had worked her way up in that bank by going to bed with that boss of hers.

He was sure Rose wouldn't have wanted her Buddhist

temple friends to know what kind of a woman she is. No! Not Mrs. Yamashiro. She's just not the type. She wouldn't even think of doing such a terrible thing.

And her boss. An upstanding community leader in Honolulu. A leader in his Christian church. A father of three children. An adulterer? No way!

Right now, he wished Reiko was there with him. To celebrate the occasion. Share a bottle of Champaign. –No, she doesn't drink. But they'd make a toast with a cup of sake for him and uron tea for her.

Reiko will be glad to know he won't have to go back to Hawaii for a nasty confrontation. Maybe he should call her. No… He better not. Her father would start wondering about them. But hell, they're just good friends. A teacher and his student.

He stepped into the kitchen, opened the small refrigerator, and took out a bottle of beer. He just couldn't restrain himself from making a toast to himself.

"Here's to you, Bruddah!" he congratulated himself. "Aloha nui loa." And took a hefty gulp.

Sitting there at the kitchen table, taking a big gulp, he was suddenly overcome by a painful aloneness. Was this the way it's going to be from now on? No one to share moments of triumphs? Of elations? Of achievements?

Is this what all divorcees go through? Suddenly feel abandoned? Deserted? Friendless?

And if a child is involved?

Poor Carrie. She'll have to endure the stigma of divorced parents. "Irreconciable differences"? Her father and mother just couldn't get along. Or whatever the lawyer would come up with.

He took another gulp. The prospect of divorcing Rose seemed great in the beginning when he found out about her and that goddamn... But now, thinking of the 23 years they had been together, well, at least until her horizon got the best of her. Those wonderful happy days.

That first time. When he met her. Their junior year at UH. In their American literature class. Then, walking over to the library to discuss their reading assignments. Then their meetings in his car; and, at cafes. So much to talk about. To look forward to. Dreams and more dreams. In between, parties at the beaches, surfing, football and basketball games...

And that day, that graduation day, her family from Maui there, announcing to them that they plan to get married. Her family had given in by then that marrying an Okinawan wasn't all that bad. And his family's resentment against her family over the Okinawan issue forgiven and forgotten.

And when the baby was born. Where was that? Oh, yeah. Back in LA. Graduate school at UCLA. Rose's father and mother coming and staying a whole month, caring for the baby.

Then, all those birthday parties for baby Carrie. Chuckie Cheese, McDonald's, Japanese and Chinese restaurants... Tons of presents from her friends at pre-school and kindergarten.

Then Disneyland! That first time. At three. Diaper trained. Fantasyland now a reality. Talking to Snow White, to Pluto, then to Bugs Bunny. Promises not to be afraid of

Goofy. Then screams and tears when Goofy the big ugly dog approaches her and wants to speak to her. "I don't like him, Daddy! I don't like him! Make him go away!"

Finally, her favorite ride, "It's A Small, Small, Small, Small, Small World." Carrie learning all the words by the time the ride through the tunnel comes to an end. "Daddy, please, I wanna go back into the small, small world."

And singing out loud to the delight of everyone around her.

Goals, achievements, glories, the gathering with faculty friends, the celebrations at bank parties... Families getting together on Christmas, exchanging gifts; hugging, wishing each other good health and happiness. And the New Year's parties, inviting her parents over from Maui to spend the day with them, then going over to Kailua to spend the day with his folks.

And now, just when they're over the hump and could start enjoying the fruits of their labor and sacrifices... All gone. Suddenly all gone. No more. Just vague memories.

Head lowered, he felt his eyes moistening.

Then tears rolling down his cheeks.

Jeesus! It's just ain't fair! To have the balloon burst just when it's ready to soar up into the skies.

Whattahell happened? Why did she start stepping out on you? You never ever did that to her.

My fault? Not paying enough attention to her? Ignoring her? Taking things for granted?

He went over to the refrigerator and opened another bottle of beer.

He stood there at the table, took a big gulp, and let his

mind wander into the happy days again.

Yeah. Those days. Those happy promising days. In a small, small world all of their own.

Then, wink of an eye and all suddenly gone. Nothing to show for 'em.

Except, of course, Carrie. The only good thing that came out of the marriage.

He hoped Carrie will never find out the real reason for their divorce. "Irreconcilable Differences," should be grounds enough. Without details.

His life without Carrie would really be empty. Their father-daughter relationship was always full of warmth, love and devotion to each other. They hardly kept secrets from each other. Not since she was a child. During her high school days, she confided in him about her dates and boys she liked or disliked. That night for her prom, he bought her the biggest orchid corsage there was at the florist. And drove her and her date to the hotel where the ceremony and party were taking place.

So many fond memories. Of him and Carrie. Will he lose her because he's divorcing her mother? Will her mother convince her that the divorce is his fault? That he's a bastard for leaving them?

"Oh, Carrie. Please remember Daddy. Daddy still loves you. Always will."

He wiped his eyes.

The phone rang.

He let it ring.

It kept ringing. And ringing.

Finally, "Hello…Ah, moshi moshi…"

"Did I get you up?"

It was Reiko.

"Oh, hi. I was in another world for a moment."

'Back with us now?" Laughter.

"Yeah. Yeah, I'm back in the real world now." Laughter, too.

"I want to thank you again for the wonderful dinner," she said.

"And the great time."

"Hey," he said, "It's I who should thank you. —Oh, by the way, I still owe you a tank of gas."

"My car runs on water." More laughter.

"You better not share your secret," he said, 'the gas companies will get after you."

"The gas companies," she said, "they should all go to jail for charging us so much."

"I'll talk to the King of Saudi Arabia," he said.

"I'll go with you."

"Okay, we'll fly over tomorrow."

Laughter.

"Chris, were you really sleeping?"

"Nah. I usually read until midnight. Besides, tonight is a special night."

"Oh?"

"Got some good news from back home."

"About your daughter?"

"Her mother."

"Good news? About her?"

"Can't get any better."

Pause.

"Chris, can I come over? My mother made andagis, and she wants you to have some."

"Okinawan donuts?"

"They're much better when they're nice and hot."

"Yes. Of course. Andagis are always much better nice and hot."

"I'll be right over."

"I'll be waiting."

Wanting to share the good news with her, he waited patiently. She sure is a good kid, he thought. And smart. And always good company.

Hey, man, he cautioned himself. She's just a young college kid. Like most of them, attracted to her professor. She's much more mature than others her age; nevertheless, still a kid.

Did she say she had a boyfriend or two? Or were they just good friends? Pretty as she is, she can have her choice. And probably will. Someday. When she's ready and willing to give herself to someone.

No. She's not the type. Okinawan college girls seemed different from American college girls. Not as sexually liberal. Not willing to go to bed with just anyone. Or doing it in a car.

Has she ever? he speculated. Gone to bed with her boyfriend or boyfriends? Nah, not her. Just not the type. That's what he had thought of Rose, too. Until she admitted she was not a virgin and was willing to before they got married.

But Reiko is not Rose. As different as a thoroughbred from a jackass. She's not a bitch in heat like Rose. She's just a clean-cut kid. Who deserved the best. A young boy with a great future like herself.

Waiting, he again thought of the good old days back home. Farrington High. Then UH. Swimming scholarship. No tuitions. Trips to the Mainland for swimming meets. And once even to Japan. Competing against the best in the relays. Yeah. He was pretty good in the relays. Broke the school record, his team.

Then hating swimming afterwards. Always reminded him of the rigid and strict training rules and hours. Never fun. Always competing. It was only during his junior year when he met Rose and spent days down at the beach that he enjoyed swimming for the first time.

One of these days, he and Reiko could go to one of the many beautiful beaches in Okinawa and spend the day swimming and sunbathing. It'd give him a chance to surprise Reiko what a great swimmer he is. "For an old man," he'd say.

And, of course, she'd say, "Oh, Chris, you're not that old." And she'd be right. He could still swim a mile at a fast clip without exhausting himself. Or, walk a mile at a fast cadence and still be able to walk another mile. "No, he's not that old."

He went back into the bedroom-office, turned on the computer to the e-mail from Douglas, and read it again. He just wanted to be sure the message was loud and clear and unambiguous.

Douglas' message was as certain as the sun rising in the east. Rose is willing to go along. Even though she thought he and Douglas were sonsofbitches, bastards and perverts.

"Sticks and stones…"

A twinge of pain and guilt stabbed him thinking of Rose looking at the pictures of her and her boss getting into and out of the hotel room. "A picture is worth a thousand words…" And Rose, poor Rose, trying to deny it. He was glad he wasn't there with Douglas to confront her.

No matter what, she is still Carrie's mother. And had shared her life with him for over 23 years. A divorce wasn't going to change any of that. She'd be a part of his life forever. All those happy days, all those sad days, all the grieving over the death of loved ones, all the rejoicings over the birth of loved ones. And any writing on a piece of paper isn't going to change that.

He thought he heard steps. He held a breath waiting for a knock on the door. The steps passed his door.

Hey, man, he said to himself. You're acting like a kid on his first date. And chuckled. Actually, he had never been on a date since those days with Rose. Here he is now, forty-four years old, waiting for a young girl of twenty-two to come knocking on his door. Not even a date.

Her mother and her father, do they approve of their daughter coming to his apartment this late in the evening? Well, why not? He is, after all, her professor. They probably consider him an uncle to her. Not an Ojii-chan grandfather; but an Oji-san uncle.

Another sound of someone walking outside.

He held another breath.

At last, a knock on the door.

He quickly turned off the computer, went over to the door, and opened it as unexcitingly as possible.

"Oh, hi. It's you."

"Hi. Were you expecting someone else?" she said.

"Yeah," he said. "People from the gas company wanting to know how to run a car on water."

She laughed that innocent laugher of hers, and, taking off her zoris, stepped in with a brown paper bag.

She was in casual jeans and a white blouse that was buttoned to her neck.

"From my mom," she said, offering the paper bag. "It's still nice and hot."

"That's how I like my andagis," he said, accepting, opening the bag. "Ah… It sure smells good."

"Go ahead. Have one."

He dug into the bag and brought out a round donut-without-holes. He took a quick bite, then another. "Boy, it sure is good, homemade andagis. Want one?"

"No. No thanks. I already had one."

He finished the first one, and brought out another one. "I hope it won't upset my stomach. Andagis with beer."

As he kept eating, she asked curiously, "What was the good news from back home?"

"You won't believe this. Douglas, my attorney, convinced Rose—that's my wife—to settle out of court. Or else we'll go to court and bring out some dirty laundry."

"Dirty laundry?

"Skeletons in the closet."

"Like Halloween?"

Chris laughed. "Yeah. Like Halloween. Only it's not funny ."

"She's willing to give you a divorce?"

Chris nodded. "Finally."

"Oh, Chris...!" She stepped forward, was about to put her arms around his neck, then backed off. "I'm so glad for you."

He instinctively opened his arms, then dropped them.

"That means you won't have to go back to Honolulu," she said.

"No," he said, "no, I can keep staying here and let the attorney handle everything over there."

"Aren't you relieved? Happy?"

"I...don't look happy?"

"Well, yes. But a little puzzled. Not really knowing how to accept the good news."

"It came so...unexpectedly. You know... I...had to digest it."

"I'm sure you're making the right decision."

"I...hope so..."

"...Well, I better go. I still have a little time left tonight to work on the translation."

"Coming along okay?'

"Coming to where I really have to get into Ojii-chan's mind."

"I'm sure you'll be able to handle it."

"Well," she said again, "I better go." She did not back off this time. Stepping forward, she put her arms around his neck and kissed his cheek lightly. "Goodnight..."

He held her for a moment, then quickly let go.

"Please thank you mother for the andagis."

"She'll be glad to know you're enjoying them."

As she stepped out of the door, he stood there, his hand

on his cheek, still feeling the warmth of her soft delicate lips.

Chapter 15: Turmoil

Driving home to Nishihara, Reiko was still in shock. She had actually kissed Chris! My goodness, Reiko! What made you do such a thing? Of course, you're good friends. But... Still... He's not one of the boys you used to date in Hawaii and kissed them "good night." He's your college professor!

Why, yes. Of course, she's drawn to him. All the girls in the class, including herself, think he's very manly and handsome. And very intelligent and worldly. She, well, she finds him to be... fascinating and...attractive and...so much more mature than the young boys she used to date. Still, she shouldn't have kissed him. What made her do that? Okinawa isn't Hawaii where everyone kisses each other, "Aloha, hello. Aloha, goodbye."

Oh, why is she making such a big thing about it? It was just a casual kiss on the cheek. Born and raised in Hawaii, he surely regards a kiss nothing more than just a custom. As a bow is to a Japanese.

She hoped he didn't think how terribly forward and aggressive she was. She was so happy for him, his wife finally agreeing to a divorce after making him go through so many confrontations. She just wanted to express her own happiness for him.

She wondered what would have happened if she had

held him a little longer and kissed him on his lips. Not casually; not passionately; just a nice warm kiss that bound them together for that moment.

Oh, Reiko! How terrible of you! He's not even divorced yet. Getting involved with another woman, any woman, is the last thing he wants happening to him right now.

Nearing home, she warned herself to stop thinking of Chris and start concentrating on Ojii-chan's Chronicle.

Parking, she suddenly wondered if Chris thought she was that kind of a girl. Easy. Willing. Thought nothing of it.

Would he believe her if she told him she had not gone to bed with a man yet? That she is still a virgin? Oh, Reiko! It's none of his business. Or any other man's business. She's saving herself for the right man and will keep saving herself until that right man comes along.

She took off her zoris at the doorway and went up the steps into her home. She was about to pass the living room when her father, watching a TV program with her mother, called, "Reiko, there's a letter for you. From Honolulu."

She stepped into the living room. "From Honolulu?"

It was from Jimmy.

"Did Yamashiro sensei like the andagis?" her mother asked.

"He loved them," she said. "He said to be sure to thank you."

As she stepped out of the room and headed toward her bedroom, she could hear her father saying to her mother, "Those two are getting pretty close, aren't they?"

"He's alone here in Okinawa," said her mother. "He must be lonely."

Reiko opened her bedroom door and stepped into her quiet private sanctuary. She opened the letter.

Dear Reiko:

You've been gone only a few weeks, but Hitoshi and I miss you something awful. It's now just a twosome without you. We went to a play the other night at the university theatre. Then to our famous café on King Street. Remember? Julie's? Without you the food was not the same. Something was missing. You.

This is going to be a short letter. Just to let you know that Hitoshi and I have been accepted at the Tokyo School of Arts. Partial scholarship. Hitoshi for music; me for painting. We are, of course, planning to fly down to Okinawa as soon as we can to visit you. Sounds okay?

We miss you and love you.

JIMMY

Oh, Jimmy, she thought. It'd be so great to be with him again.

Tokyo School of Arts! An American going there! What an honor. But, then, Jimmy was practically a Nihonjin *Japanese* anyway. Being with Hitoshi would help him get adjusted to the Tokyo life.

She told herself to get back to Ojii-chan's Chronicle. She had finished her class studies at the university library earlier today and was now free to work on the Chronicle. It was taking her longer than she had expected. Her eagerness to come to the last part, however, drove her on.

Sitting at her desk, she gathered the clipped papers of the last translated chapter and read them. It was okay. But needed more work. She'd work on it and the other chapters when she transcribed them into the computer and printed them. The hardest part was the transitions from one chapter to the next. To connect Ojii-chan's thoughts, intentions and dialogues.

She began:

Franky and his outfit had been gone for over a week, and we did not know what happened to them. We did not think we'd ever see Franky again. We could only hope that he is fine and would one day return home safely to America.

The replacement POW guards were younger. They watched and treated us as criminals. Which, in a way, we were. I'm sure they, like us, wished the war was over, and we could all return home.

There was no question in my mind by then that we could not win the war. The Americans were superior in many ways. We could not match their battleships, their airplanes, their tanks and their countless Army, Navy and Marine Forces. And their dedication and loyalty to their country were as strong as ours were to our Emperor.

Whenever our families from Ie Jima came to visit us and spoke to us through the fences, we learned more and more of the thousands of Uchinanchus being killed in the battlefronts with the Japanese soldiers. Why aren't they fleeing up to the northern mountains like many of them from central and southern Okinawa were doing? If they can't, why aren't they surrendering to the Americans? Surely they must know by now that the Americans are not the barbarians we've been told they are.

The last time Obaa-chan came to visit me (we were not married yet) she told me about Hidenobu, our neighbor's young sixteen-year-old-boy, who attacked an American Marine squad with grenades and was killed instantly. Hidenobu, like other young boys his age, wanted to be a hero. Now his father and mother don't have a son to carry on their family name.

Reiko, as before, when reading the Japanese version, cringed and shook her head. So young! So innocent! So brainwashed!

She continued on.

We heard by now that Shuri Castle was gone. It was leveled by the powerful guns of the American battleships anchored at the bay. Thousands of our people who labored for the Japanese Army and who actually fought with them were either killed, captured, or buried in the underground tunnels of the castle. Ushijima Taisho and thousands of his soldiers were now in Mabuni, holed up in caves and fighting to the last man.

So sad, I thought, fighting a war that could not be won. We knew that Okinawa was being sacrificed to give the Mainland the needed time to prepare for the invasion by the American forces. We also knew it was the Emperor's wish that we Okinawans sacrifice ourselves for the sake of all Japan. The Nipponjins on the Mainland, we heard, were willing to fight the invading Americans with knives and spears. The battles on the Mainland would involve millions of Nipponjins and millions of Americans and could go on forever.

Life seemed so meaningless, I thought. So sacrificial, so temporary and so short-lived. Is this why we were born? Raised? To attain a certain age and give it up for a cause that was still foreign to most of us? We've heard about the Emperor since childhood. That he was Kami Sama God to all of us. No one, much less us Uchinanchus, had ever seen him. If he is Kami Sama, why is he letting thousands of us in Okinawa and millions of Nipponjins in the Mainland suffer so horribly? To die so senselessly?

I was only eighteen then. Not worldly, not educated, certainly not wise, just a young man with endless time to think of the many things that have happened to him. I was now a one-legged POW, no longer able to serve his country; perhaps, now a liability to his country and to his people. I had seen deaths and had experienced my own near-death. All I had learned so far was that life is especially precious when you are about to lose it.

I now wanted to know the reason for my existence. Why was I spared when my companions were not? All the important things up until now seemed unimportant and all the unimportant things now suddenly important. Foremost among the important were self-discovery and spiritual values.

I knew nothing about rediscovering myself; I could only search for it. I knew nothing about my enemies and I was supposed to have killed one of them. Now, I was at peace with myself for not having done that. For not having taken away the precious life of a fellow human being.

I had met a former enemy who had become a friend. And I had learned much from him. That we, after all, are all brothers. Brothers who were taught to hate each other until discovering that love conquers all; not hatred.

During one of Obaa-chan's visits, she told me of an American grave that was below Gusuku Yama. It was strange, she said, that there should be a grave for a single American soldier when many more had been killed. She said there were words printed on a piece of crude lumber standing near the grave, which she could not read nor understand.

I, of course, had heard of this man from Franky. The man was not a soldier but a newspaper reporter. Franky and his GI friends were angry and sad that Ernie Pyle had been killed when he had been there just to write about the invasion of Ie Jima.

It was terrible, I thought, that this famous newspaper man who did not carry a weapon was killed by one of our soldiers. Couldn't he see Ernie Pyle was just a civilian newspaper reporter who meant no harm to anyone?

If Ernie Pyle was loved by an American GI like Franky, he must have been a good man, I said to myself. A great man! Who would be missed not only by GIs but by all the people in America.

I told Obaa-chan that when she goes back home to Ie Jima, she should place a bouquet of flowers at Ernie-san's grave and to burn osenkos for Ernie-san's spirit.

When Obaa-chan came back the following week, she said that when she did what I told her to do, several GIs visiting the grave thanked her for the flowers. The GIs did not really know what the osenkos meant, but was grateful when she put her hands together and prayed for Ernie-san's spirit.

When Obaa-chan asked me why we were doing this for Ernie-san, I really did not know why myself. Except, perhaps, to honor a man who was loved and cherished by all his countrymen.

One day, I told myself, when the war is over, I must get to know more about Ernie-san. Especially since he was buried on my island and people would want to know about him. By that time there might be books written about him. Of course, it would be in English which I could read a little and would be able to read much better after I went back to high school.

I still had a year more left for my high school diploma. Now that I was disabled, I had no choice but to go back to school. I could no longer be a fisherman like my father or be a laborer in *the sugarcane fields. It would be best for me to become a schoolteacher. I could learn English and teach it to my students. When the war is over, and it should end soon, there will be a need for Uchinanchus to know English. Americans, I was sure, would occupy Okinawa for years to come and knowing English would be important.*

If one day Okinawa should have a university I could go there and get a degree. And, maybe, become a university professor. Yes. That would be great. Me, a university professor.

I may be a disabled, one-legged man, but that does not make me a mentally disabled man, I said to myself. It would, on the other hand, drive me to read more and to learn more about what is going on in the world. Especially about this war. Why did we get involved in it? What made us think we could defeat a great and mighty country like America? What prompted us to attack Pearl Harbor in Hawaii when we were still fighting China?

Yes, there is much to learn. To prepare myself to teach English to my students about America and about Americans like Franky and Ernie-san.

So that's what made Ojii-chan become an educator, Reiko said to herself when she first read the Chronicle. He received his high school diploma, then, eventually, when there was a university in Okinawa, went on to get a degree. He did not become a professor, but had become a teacher at Nakijin High School. And had also become a famous English lecturer throughout the different high schools and universities.

According to what Reiko read, his lectures were almost always about the tragedies of the Okinawan battles and how Uchinanchus until then had not been considered loyal

Nipponjins. The ultimate sacrifices made by Uchinanchus, he declared, were the result of their belief in Yamato Damashii, the soul of Japan.

At first, Reiko wondered why Ojii-chan had not written his Chronicle in English. He might have written it much better than she struggling to translate it. As she kept reading and working on the original version, she realized that Ojii-chan's Japanese was much more expressive and much more sincere than had he written it in English. There were Japanese words, insights and observations that could not be expressed adequately in English as they could be in Japanese.

And it was her responsibility to replace Ojii-chan's Japanese with English words and phrases, which seemed impossible at first, but was now becoming a little easier.

There were a few contradictions here and there. Most notably was Ojii-chan's loyalty and belief in Yamato Damashii. Yet, he saw its failure, its blinding indoctrination that led to thousands of unnecessary suicides and deaths.

According to his Chronicle he always concluded his lectures with afterthoughts that no one really won the battle of Okinawa. How can America declare victory when so many of its young men perished in the battlefields? How can Japan speak of Yamato Damashii when thousands of its soldiers suffered their fates so terribly?

Reiko, who was born over two generations after the war, hardly knew anything about what the older Uchinanchus went through during and right after the war. All she heard from them was "Minna kuroshita." *Everyone suffered terribly.*

Ojii-chan, himself, hardly spoke of his own experience in the war. Not even how he lost his leg. Or anything connected with it. His sacrifice was "Shikata Ga Nai." *It couldn't be helped.* A Japanese philosophical saying that was impossible to truly express in English.

She went on to the next chapter.

One day, out of nowhere, came a Nisei interpreter in our POW camp. He was, from what we could gather, a Hawaii born Japanese-American. He was in his early twenties, quite tall for a Japanese, and spoke with a peculiar accent. His Japanese was bookish, practiced and recited. He had several stripes on his sleeves and interrogated many of us in a hot, stifling shack trying to find out how many more Japanese soldiers were in central and northern Okinawa. And if so, where are they hiding?

We would not have given him that information even if we knew. Which, of course, we did not. He screamed at us across the table in the shack for withholding information that would cost thousands of lives, both Japanese and Americans.

When he interrogated me the second time, he seemed sympathetic because of my missing leg. "Didn't the American military doctors treat you well?" he asked. "Didn't they save your other leg?" I was being treated like a child, I thought. "You can now help us save thousands of lives by giving us the information we need." I agreed with him, but could not give him the information. How could I?

"Listen," he said, looking at me across the table, "I am a Nihonjin like you. I don't want to see more of you killed. You can help us stop the killings by telling us where those soldiers are."

Again, how can I give him information I did not have?

Controlling himself, he said, "You Okinawans, why are you fighting for a country that looks down on you? Considers you inferior? Regards you as Chinese rather than Nihonjins?"

This Nisei, I told myself, he knows nothing about our history; about how we became Nipponjins. Yes, he is in a nice, clean striped American Army uniform, but how can he think he is better than me when his parents who emigrated from somewhere in Japan, were once poor peasants. Isn't it just an accident, I told myself, that he is sitting there with a revolver in his buckle while I sit across from him in my ragged one-legged pants and a shredded shirt?

I began to hate this proud, arrogant Japanese-American. He was worse than the proud, arrogant Nipponjins from the Mainland who sometimes treated us as inu dogs. The fate of the mainland Nippon-jin soldiers were at least the same as ours. This Nisei who keeps staring at me thinks his parents were upper class, educated Nihonjins when they really were simple, uneducated peasants who went to work in the sugar cane fields.

"What's your name?" *he questioned, calming himself.*

I did not answer.

"Your name is a secret, too?" *he said.*

I remained silent.

"We saved your life and this is how you cooperate?"

I stood up with my crutches. "Can I leave now?"

The proud Nisei jumped up and slammed his hand down hard on the table. "Sit down!"

I kept standing with my crutches.

"I said, sit down!"

I defiantly sat back down.

We sat across from each other, just staring at one another.

The Nisei, I was sure, had been in battles. Well, so was I. Nothing could be more frightening than when you are about to lose your life. Exchanging stares with the proud Nisei was simply a child's game. And we were both children at the moment.

"I don't understand you," the Nisei now said, "you lost a leg for a country that now don't give a damn about you. And you still believe in it?"

I was getting tired of the game. And so I asked him one simple question. "Where are your parents from?"

He looked at me, coldly.

"Is that a secret?" I asked, keeping my eyes steadily on him.

"Where my parents came from is none of your goddamn business!" he finally said.

"Yes, I said. It is none of my business. Just thought I'd ask. Like you're asking me all your questions." Again, we looked at each other harshly.

Finally, flinging his hand toward the door, he said, "Get out of here."

"Domo arigato gozaimashita," I said, bowing low to the conquerer. "Thank you very much." And stepped out of the oppressive shack.

Although Reiko had already read this chapter, she still found Ojii-chan's defiance humorous and audacious. The chapter was especially interesting in that it revealed a facet of Ojii-chan she did not know.

Her eyelids were quite heavy now, her mind not as incisive as an hour ago. She placed her pen on the desk, rubbed her eyes and rearranged the translated pages. The following chapter, she said to herself, will give an ever deeper revelation of Ojii-chan's insightful observations of the war.

Before rising from her chair and calling it a night, she suddenly remembered what happened at Chris' apartment. She was still shocked over it. But not as much as when she first left the apartment. Chris probably expected it, she told herself. And, besides, he held her, too, didn't he?

Oh, Reiko!

Chapter 16: Solitude

When Chris heard Reiko's steps receding toward the elevator, he kept standing there at the door his hand still on his cheek, not wanting the feel of her warm delicate lips to evaporate.

He could hear the rumbling of the elevator stopping, the door opening, shutting, and the elevator finally dropping to the lower floors.

He wished she could have stayed a little longer. Keep him company. Celebrate with him the occasion of the news from Douglas.

He forced himself to step away from the door, his hand gradually lowering away from his cheek.

Jeesus Ca-rist, Chris! She's just a kid. One of your students.

He shook his head, shaking off the pretty image of Reiko before him. Hey, man. Knock it off. You're jumping from the frying pan into the fire.

He returned to his bedroom-office, turned on the computer to his e-mails, expecting more news from Douglas. There was none. He brought up the latest letter. He read it again. To make sure he had not missed anything. Or to make sure what he read was actually what Douglas had sent.

Relieved, he e-mailed Douglas.

Thanks for the good news, Douglas. No one could have handled it better. I'm sure neither of us wanted a nasty protracted trial. The grounds, I believe will be 'Irreconcilable Differences.' Right? We can both go on with our lives now.

Mahalo nui loa.

Chris.

Now that he and Rose would no longer be married, he again felt a painful loneliness gripping him. Not only because he would not be seeing her anymore, unless accidentally, but not being able to talk about the many things they used to share. Especially about Carrie.

Twenty-three years gone. All gone!

He was already forty-four. Will he ever meet someone like Rose again when she was that unpretentious Maui country girl? Or was he destined to be a lonely bachelor the rest of his life?

Hey, man! Forty-four ain't so old. There's still lotsa life left in you. Rose found herself a lover. Why can't you?

No matter what you still have Carrie. She'd always be your girl. Even Rose can't deny that.

He'd better snap out of it. He had a class to lecture tomorrow morning. The kids deserve a dedicated professor, not a mourning one. He'd better be prepared to discuss in detail James Jones' "From Here To Eternity," and make it interesting.

Next morning, he ate a couple of the andagis Reiko had brought over, downed a cup of hot coffee, and was on a forty-five-minute bus ride to Ryudai. He missed the drive from his home in Manoa Valley to the UH campus, the high mountains on both sides of the valley always cool, misty and green. The bus ride, however, gave him an elevated view of the colorful Okinawan cities and the blue-green China Sea on the western shores.

In the classroom, where the students had left their shoes and slippers outside, he found himself looking for Reiko. She was usually there before him in one of the front seats. Then, the door opened, and she came in smiling that pretty girlish smile of hers.

"Sorry for being late, Sensei," she said, bowing apologetically. A little car trouble."

"Everything okay now?"

"Hai."

She was in a cotton aloha blouse and a Levi skirt emphasizing her slim figure. A picture of a UH coed. Which made him feel a little homesick.

Several of the students who were given condensed chapters of "From Here To Eternity" had already discussed their version of the novel, and had done a pretty good job. One of the girl students, Mari, was especially interested in what happened to the Japanese-American girl, Violet, who was the girlfriend of the main character Prew. When Chris explained why Violet and Prew stopped their relationship, Mari thought it was so sad that they did not get married. Chris, again, had to explain that the story took place long ago and Americans did not marry Japanese in those days.

Seikichi, a boy student who was assigned a chapter well into the novel was intrigued and surprised that there were so many white American prostitutes in Hawaii.

Mari said she also loved the relationship between Sergeant Warden and the Captain's wife, Karen Holmes. It is a beautiful warm love story, she said. One just a soldier, the other an officer's wife. Both of them willing to jeopardize their lives for each other's love.

Mitsuo, another boy student, thought Prew was truly a great character throughout the story. Prew was willing to give up his position as a bugler and would not join the boxing team because he was against the Army establishment. He was anti-Army yet loved the Army life. Which made him by far the most intriguing character in the novel.

Chris was glad that the students were getting into the story. He was afraid the book was too long and complicated. A pre-Pearl Harbor and post-Pearl Harbor book may not be interesting for them.

Sachiko, one of the girls sitting up front with Reiko, said she saw the movie "From Here To Eternity" and loved it. Except for the love affair of Prew and his prostitute girlfriend, Alma. The book was interesting because it felt real. Whereas the movie did not show the real life of a Honolulu prostitute.

Again, Chris was happy that the students were captivated by the novel.

Reiko, not saying anything until now, said, "Chris... Sensei, why don't you tell them about the places mentioned in downtown Honolulu?"

"You mean Beretania Street and Hotel Street?" Chris said.

"And River Street and Aala Park," said Reiko.

"Well," Chris said, "they're not what they used to be. They've been cleaned up. Prostitution is no longer legal in

Hawaii. The long lines of GIs and sailors out on the sidewalks waiting for their turn to go upstairs are things of the past."

"You mean the GIs and sailors waited in lines for their turn?" said Sumiko, a girl in the back, shocked.

"You've gotta realize," said Chris, "all the young servicemen were away from home for the first time. And they found Hawaii a romantic paradise, but not enough girls."

"And so they went to those places?" said Sumiko.

"What better place to go in paradise?" said Mitsuo, and chuckled.

"I heard there was a time here in Okinawa during the early days of the occupation when the American servicemen waited for their turns in the villages," said Seikichi.

"Koza Village was famous for that," said a boy who had been silent and whose name Chris had forgotten.

"They called it four-corners Koza," joined another boy.

"How do you know that?" said Mari. "You were not even born yet."

"I heard about it," replied the boy. 'I also heard that the black GIs went to one corner of Koza, the white GIs the other. If they crossed the corners, they would be a fight among them."

"Okay, okay," Chris interrupted, "we're getting off the subject," and stopped the talk about four-corners Koza.

"Sensei," said Mitsuo, "what is really interesting about 'Eternity' is the how the soldiers got along or did not get along with each other."

"You mean the relationship among themselves?" said Chris.

"Hai," said Mitsuo. "Here in Okinawa we see the uniforms of the servicemen; not the person wearing the uniform. In 'Eternity' we see the soldiers as real people. What they like, what they don't like, who they like, who they don't like. We see them as human beings; not just figures in uniform like here in Okinawa."

"It's because most of you don't take the trouble to get to know the servicemen here," said Chris.

"It's because the servicemen don't care to get to know us," said Mitsuo. "They know nothing of our ways, our interests, our wants. They look at us and think we're just a bunch of foreigners."

"The servicemen during the days of 'Eternity' were not really accepted by the people of Hawaii," Chris stuck to 'Eternity.' "Girls who went out with them were considered tramps and low class by the locals."

"Even though they were white Americans?" said Sumiko.

"Most of the soldiers in Hawaii were there because they couldn't find jobs in America," Chris explained. "This was during the Great Depression. Joining the Army at least offered them a roof over their heads and three meals a day.

"It is a very interesting period in American History," he went on. "In Hawaii, there were always jobs working in the canefields or the pineapple fields. It was hard work, but you had a little income coming in. In Mainland America, people were lining up in soup lines, depending on the government and Salvation Army and the Red Cross for food."

"That's why many of them joined the Army or the Navy?" asked Mitsuo.

"It was better than begging for food," said Chris. "And so the servicemen in Hawaii those days, even though they were white Americans, or haoles as the locals called them, were of the poor and struggling class."

"Here in Okinawa," said Mitsuo, "we think that the American servicemen all come from educated, well-to-do families. In 'Eternity' we see them as ordinary young men trying to find a place for themselves. They are real men, struggling and fighting among themselves, ordering the low class and taking orders from the higher class, wanting to advance and better themselves while others are trying to hold them down…"

"I read that James Jones, the author of 'Eternity,' went through the things he wrote about," said Seikichi. "That's why the book is so real. He wrote the book exactly as he felt and saw everything around him."

"How can one man write all those different parts and make you believe he is that person?" Mari said. "I became all the people in the book. Prew, Sgt Warden, Captain Holmes, Karen, and even the terrible sergeant of the Army jail. They were all so real."

"That's what good writing is all about," said Chris. "When the author can make the reader forget him or herself and become the characters. And Jones was successful in doing that."

"Is he still living?" asked Mari.

"He died pretty young," said Chris. "Fifty-seven."

"Did he write other books?"

"Several more. But 'Eternity' was his best."

The discussion about 'Eternity' and Jones went on for the rest of the period. There were still several more minutes left before the bell. He told the class to keep reading and studying their assignments until then. They'd have another in-depth discussion when they meet again on Monday.

The bell rang and the class marched over to the hallway where they put on their shoes and slippers, their quiet voices now loud and rambling in Japanese.

Reiko stepped up to his desk. "I'm going to Ie Jima tomorrow. Want to come along?"

"Tomorrow?" He thought about it for a second. He didn't have anything pressing to do. "Sure," he said. "It's about time I visited that island of yours."

"I'm visiting Obaa-chan. Taking parts of Ojii-chan's Chronicle to her so she can start reading them."

"You're that far into it?"

"I'm about two-thirds done," she said. "I can't wait to finish it."

"Me, too."

"I'll pick you up tomorrow at eight, okay?"

"At eight. Right."

At the door, before putting on her shoes, she turned and said, "Be sure to bring your swimming trunks."

"We're going swimming?"

She nodded. "There's a sandy beach, my secret spot where I used to go swimming when I used to visit Ojii-chan and Obaa-chan during my high school days."

"Sounds almost like a beach on the windward side of Honolulu."

"Hardly anyone on the island goes to my secret spot," she said and went off to her next class.

He went over to his office building, got off the elevator on the third floor and stepped down the hallway toward his office. There was a note pinned on the door: "Chris, will you come over to my office, please. Takashi."

He went directly to Takashi's office, which was three doors away.

He knocked.

"Come in," said Takashi.

He opened the door and stepped in.

Takashi was at his computer, going over an e-mail. His office, as small as all the other professors', always had a coffee pot brewing. As expected, his desk was cluttered with notes, books and his latest class lecture.

"Sit here, Chris," he said, and pushed aside some of the notes and books. "Want some coffee?"

"No, no thanks," said Chris. "I had a cup in my office before class."

"How's your class doing?"

"Great. At least I think so."

"Couple of your students said they're really enjoying the book you assigned them," said Takashi, refilling his coffee cup. "Army life in Hawaii, right?"

"Yeah. Peace time Army life before the war and right after Pearl Harbor."

"I always meant to read that book, 'From Here To Eternity' when I was at UH. Just didn't have the time for it.

You know, graduate studies and all."

"The whole story takes place in Hawaii," he said. "Places I'm sure you've been or heard about."

"I'm going to make it my next novel," said Takashi, taking a long sip.

There was a pause. Chris waited for Takashi's real reason for calling him into his office.

Finally.

"I was called into the Chairman's office this morning," Takashi began.

He looked at Takashi, vague-eyed.

"The Chairman of the English Department," Takashi added.

"Professor Asato?"

Takashi nodded.

He suspected what was coming.

"Asato got word about you and Reiko," said Takashi.

For lack of any other response, he said, "Oh...?"

"I won't go into detail what Asato heard," Takashi went on. "There are always gossip mongers on campus who can't mind their own business.

"Anyway," Takashi went on, uncomfortably, "a word to the wise."

"I'm not supposed to be seen with Reiko anymore?" he said, restraining himself. "Even though we're just friends?"

"Hey, Chris. If I had it my way, you can be seen with any of your female students. Day or night. I wouldn't give a damn."

"But... University policy?"

Takashi nodded and looked away.

Chris grinned. It turned into a chortle as he shook his head.

"What if I told you that Reiko and I are not having an affair," he said.

"Hey, Chris. It's none of my business. And I wish it was none of anybody else's business, too."

Pause.

Finally. "So…"

"She's one of our top English students, Chris. She has a bright future here."

"I'd ruin her future if we keep seeing each other?"

"Ah, c'mon."

"She's been good enough to take me all over Okinawa and opened my eyes to many things I knew nothing about," Chris said.

"That's great. I'm glad for you. For both of you. But, still…?" Takashi nodded. "It's better that the Chairman stops hearing about you two."

"You, too?"

"Me? Hey, Chris, I'm personally glad you found her. She's a very attractive young girl." "Takashi," he said.

"I didn't find her. We met and somehow happened to enjoy each other's company. "…Oh, Christ," he went on. "I feel like a kid told by a girl's father to stop seeing his daughter."

"And me?" said Takashi. "How does all this make me feel?"

"Yeah, I know," he said, nodding. "Sorry you have to get involved."

"I'm not involved," said Takashi. "It's your

relationship; not mine."

"Relationship..." he muttered, chuckling, shaking his head.

"Okay," said Takashi. "I've said what I was supposed to say."

Chris rose. "Hai, Sensei."

And they both laughed.

Chapter 17: Rainstorm

Early next morning, Reiko drove over to pick up Chris. In Hawaiian beach shorts, aloha shirt and zoris, he was waiting for her at the office steps of the mansion. Reiko, reminding herself that she was no longer in Hawaii, was in jeans, T-shirt and sandals; not in her Hawaiian beach outfit. In the back seat was a picnic basket with sandwiches, water bottles, a long tropical Hawaiian beach towel and her conservative swimming outfit.

She lowered the car radio and drove over to the expressway, paid the attendant at the checkpoint, and headed north. She wanted to go through Ishikawa where Chris' grandfather and grandmother had come from, then continue driving northward. Chris knew of no relatives living in Ishikawa anymore and so there was no reason to stop there.

They got off the expressway, passed through a modern city with high concrete office and apartment buildings, then got back on the expressway. Chris was disappointed that the village his grandfather used to speak of existed only in his mind. Memories of grass-thatched shacks, unpaved mud roads, pigs and chickens occupying the yards and wells.

"Funny how impressions stay with you," Chris now said, looking back at modern Ishikawa from the expressway. "How they become a part of your life. Even when you've never been there."

Reiko glanced over at him.

"Feels you've been cheated," Chris went on. "It was there; now it's gone. Ishikawa village never changed for my grandfather. It was always the same village he had left."

"It's the same with language," Reiko said. "People speak the same way they did years after they left. In Hawaii," she went on, "the older Japanese spoke the Nihongo that was spoken during Emperor Meiji's era in the late1800s. They are not aware that times have changed. That everything, including Nihongo, has been modernized since they left their homeland."

Chris chuckled.

"You disagree?"

"Oh, no, no. Something just hit me."

"Like?"

"This Uchinanchu old man returned home to Okinawa. He had been gone over fifty years. After been back less than a year, he returned to Hawaii."

"For a visit?"

"For good. He had become a Hawaiian and didn't know it. He was mixing Hawaiian and English words with his Okinawan and Japanese words and the villagers couldn't understand him."

"I sometimes couldn't understand some of the local UH students," she said. "I would be mistaken for one of them and their pidgin English used to baffle me. "Pau," "bumby," "talk story…"

"Hey, you," Chris joined, "Pau talk story a'ready. Bumby boss come, he angry like hell. Bettah go back hana hana."

They both laughed.

Driving on from Ishikawa, now each to each's own silent thoughts, Reiko thought of Ojii-chan's Ishikawa village when he was a POW there.

The following chapter in his Chronicle continued with his encounter with the Nisei interpreter.

All the POWs, especially the Uchinanchus, had concluded that the Nisei was a Naicha whose parents emigrated to Hawaii from Mainland Japan, Ojii-chan went on. That accounted for his proud, superior attitude toward us Uchinanchus.

The Nisei continued to aim his interrogation at Uchinanchus, apparently hoping that one of us would give him the information his American superiors wanted. Except for a few of us who were actually in the Japanese Army, most of the Uchinanchu POWs were forced laborers. If we in the regular Army did not know the information the Americans wanted, how could the forced laborers know?

I began wondering if there really were Japanese Army forces in central and northern Okinawa. I had thought they were all in the southern battlefronts. If it is true that the Japanese Army were close to our POW camp, they'd be coming to rescue us. It was not a comforting thought. There would be a fierce battle with the Americans and many of us would be caught in the middle.

I was again called into the hot stifling shack.

The Nisei and I sat across the table from each other once more. I kept wondering from what prefecture his parents emigrated to Hawaii.

"So, Oshiro,'" he began, "'you've changed your mind? You're going to cooperate with us?'"

Is this another of his tricks? I said to myself.

I remained silent.

"You've volunteered to talk to me, hai?"

I was not going to be trapped by this clever Nisei, I told myself.

"'Well!"

I said nothing.

When I still remained silent, he gave me a hard cold look.

"Aren't you treated well by us!" he roared.

"Domo arigato gozaimasu," I said, bowing, eyes down on the table.

"Then?"

"I know nothing about what you want to know," I finally said. "I am sorry."

"You are sorry!" he roared again. "You're gonna be really sorry when thousands more of you Uchinanchus are killed!"

He had pronounced 'Uchinanchu,' clearly and I was surprised.

A big, tall, blue-eyed American officer entered the shack without knocking. He studied me with cold, scornful eyes, his hands balled into fists.

"Can't you get anything out of them?'" the officer said to the Nisei. I could understand at least that much of his English. The officer walked around the table and faced me.

"You!" he pointed a finger at me, "we're trying to saves lives, you understand that!?"

I looked away.

"Goddamn it! Sergeant Nakama," the officer returned to the

Nisei, "'can't you make them understand that all we want to know is whether or not there's Japanese soldiers still hiding up in the mountains."

Did he call the Nisei, 'Nakama'?

"I'm trying, Sir," said the Nisei.

"Well, try harder!" said the officer. "And get results. If none of them are left up in the mountains, we gotta move back down South and join the fighting down there."

The officer stepped back to the door. "...And Sergeant," he added, "I don't give a damn how you get the information. Just get it. Understand!"

"Yes, Sir."

So, I said to myself, still surprised. The Nisei's name is Nakama.

"From where in Okinawa are your parents from?" I asked.

The Nisei looked at me, his arrogance replaced by an annoyed, impatient looks, his eyes avoiding mine.

"There are several Nakama's where I come from," I said.

He now looked at me, probing silently.

"Where's that?" he finally asked.

"Ie Jima."

"Ie Jima," he said. "The same island Ernie Pyle was killed?"

I nodded.

"Goddamn you guys!'" he said. "'Ernie Pyle was not a soldier. He was a reporter.. He never carried a rifle; just his pencil and paper.'"

I said nothing.

"You guys killed a guy who was a hero to every one of us."

I thought of what Franky had said about Ernie-san and was

now more convinced that if Ernie-san was a hero to this Nisei, too, he must have been a hero to everyone, Americans as well as non-Americans.

"Maybe it was one of you goddamn POWs who shot him," the Nisei said bitterly. "He better not let me get hold of him!" the Nisei warned, pointing his trigger finger at me.

The Nisei still had not told me where his parents were from.

"Your father and mother..."

The Nisei did not hesitate this time. "Nago."

"Ah, so. Nago. I went to high school with Nakama, Tamotsu, in Motobu. His home was in Nago."

"The only relative I know of is my father's brother, Yasukazu Nakama."

"Nakama, Yasukazu... I don't think I know him."

"'I was hoping he was one of you,'" said the Nisei. "'I checked all the POWs here."

"If you want me, to," I said, "I can ask around to see if anyone knows or heard of your uncle."

The Nisei nodded, gratefully.

"If he's over forty years old," I said, "he wouldn't be in the Army.

"I hope not," the Nisei said. "I don't want to end up shooting my my own uncle."

"No." I said. "That wouldn't be right."

"Listen," said the Nisei, "you telling me the truth? You don't know of Japanese soldiers up here?"

I shook my head emphatically. "If there were," I said, "I would have heard about it."

He looked at me and believed me. And I believed that if there were any of our soldiers up in the mountains we would have *heard about them.*

After a moment of silence, I could not resist asking, "How come you, a Japanese, is in the American Army?"

"I am an American," the Nisei said.

"Yes, I guess you are," I said. "But why are you fighting against the country of your father and mother?"

"Because the country of my father and mother attacked my country."

"And your father and mother said it is all right for you to fight against Japan?"

"They said it is all right to fight for a country I believed in."

"You don't think Japan is your country, too?"

"I look like you; you look like me. But here," he pointed to his heart, "we are different."

"Because of that uniform?"

"Because I was taught to be an American all my life."

"Yes, of course," I said, still not quite understanding the Nisei.

"You must have heard of the old samurai story about a boy adopted by another family," the Nisei said. "'When the two families fought each other, the adopted boy had to fight against his own blood father and brothers."

"Yes," I said, "I've heard of that story. But in those days, they took a loyalty oath dedicating their lives to their samurai family."

"The same as the loyalty oath I took when I joined the American Army," the Nisei said.

"And the American soldiers trusted you?"

"I am the same as them, an American soldier."

"Yes," I said. "Yes, I guess you are."

After another moment of silence, I asked, "Did you kill any of your own people?"

"Nihonjins?"

"Uchinanchus."

"I don't know if I killed anyone," said the Nisei. "All I know I shot at them when they attacked us."

"Here in Okinawa?

"Saipan."

"There's lots of Uchinanchus in Saipain," I said.

"That's what I found out."

"And you shot them!?"

"The Japanese soldiers; not the civilians."

It just did not sound right, two Japanese soldiers shooting at each other.

"We tried to stop the Uchinanchus from committing suicide," the Nisei went on. "They were told by the goddamn Japanese soldiers it's better to die than to be captured by American soldiers."

"That's what we were told by our leaders, too," I said.

"'Look at you today," he said. "You never had it better."

I nodded gratefully. "Except for losing one of my legs."

"You still have your other leg."

"Yes," I said, "yes, I still have my other leg."

"Did you kill any of us Americans?" he asked.

I shook my head. "I don't think so."

"'You never shot at us?"

"I don't remember."

"You don't remember?"

"Several artillery shells landed on our pillbox and killed five of us," I said. "I survived. My right leg was almost gone and the *blood from my head was blinding me."*

I, of course, did not tell him that I had tried to kill Americans with one of our battered machine guns.

"Then you were saved by our medics?"

Again, I nodded gratefully.

The Nisei now cursed, *"This goddamn war! First, we try to kill them; then we try to save 'em..."*

"It puzzles me, too" I said.

The Nisei took his pack of cigarettes from his shirt pocket, fingered one out and stuck it between his lips. Before lighting it he took out another, offered it to me, lit mine then his.

"Domo arigato gozaimasu," I said, *and inhaled deeply, appreciatively.*

The Nisei stood up from the table and extended his hand across it. I was, of course, surprised. I reached over, shook his hand in both of mine and bowed respectfully.

Reiko was glad that Ojii-chan had discovered the Nisei was an Uchinanchu and that the Nisei's arrogance had mellowed somewhat. They had not reconciled. They, after all, were still enemies. But their spirits and hearts were those of Uchinanchus who loved and respected the land of their ancestors.

After a few more miles northward, Reiko headed westward over the mountains to the China Sea coast. She turned the radio a little louder and the Okinawan music could be heard over the humming of the car engine and the whirring of tire sounds.

Chris finally awoke.

"Had a nice nap?" she said, lowering the radio a notch.

"Sorry," he said. "Didn't mean to fall asleep."

Rubbing his eyes, he looked out the window curiously.

"We're going through the mountains toward Nago," she said. "We'll be looking toward the China Sea in a few more minutes."

Chris was now enjoying the scenic drive through tall green pines, lush wild flowers along the roadside and the view of the Pacific Coast behind them.

The music was cut off and the latest news came on. A heavy rainstorm that started near the Philippines was on its way up north toward Taiwan and Okinawa.

"Oh, oh," she said.

"What did he say?" Chris asked.

"A heavy rainstorm coming up our way."

"We're still heading for the beach?"

"As long as it's not a typhoon, we're okay," Reiko said.

They could finally see the China Sea unfolding before them.

"I hope to go through a typhoon before I go back home," Chris said.

"Just to say you've gone through an Okinawan typhoon?" Reiko said.

"A good conversation piece."

"Yes. When it's all over."

"Pretty bad, huh? Trees toppling over; roofs blown away; cars turned over… I don't think anyone wants to go through that."

"Okay, okay," Chris said. "I take it back. I hope I won't go through an Okinawan typhoon."

The sparkling China Sea coastline was still calm, unpassed by the upcoming rainstorm. Up front, to the left, was the colorful city of Nago, above it on the hillside, majestic buildings, several of them the newly built campus of Meio University.

Chris, she noticed, was impressed by the western coast of the island, so unlike the staid, unimpressive eastern coast line. "Is that Ie Jima?" he asked, pointing to the tiny island off the Motobu coast.

"That's it," she replied. "We'll get on a ferry and go across the bay."

"Looks small," he said. "And that mountain…?"

"Mt. Gusuku."

"Everything else is so flat."

"The mountain is six hundred feet high with tunnels under it, " Reiko said.

"Can't believe that a great writer like Ernie Pyle was killed on a small and insignificant island like that."

They finally arrived at the harbor where a ferry was waiting to take sightseers, tourists and island residents to Ie Jima.

Reiko drove the car onto the ferry, got off and led Chris up the stairway to the next passenger's deck. The TV was on in the room and again the main news was the forthcoming rainstorm. It said that the rainstorm was not heading directly toward Okinawa, but was sure to hit the western part of the island a little after sunset.

It was still mid-morning and Reiko was not too concerned about the storm. They'd be back to the safety of their home before then.

Driving out of the ferry, she headed toward Mt. Gusuku the tall pinnacle of a mountain looming overhead from whichever spot on the island. She climbed up to the parking space at the foot of the mountain where concessionaires were selling island-grown peanuts, papayas and imported soda pops and ice cream.

From the elevated parking lot they could see clearly Motobu, Nago and the small towns on the opposite shorelines. Behind them was the pinnacle, beckoning them.

"We better not climb to the top today," Reiko said. "Maybe next time when we have more time."

"I was looking forward to it," Chris said, bending his knees, stretching his legs and arms, taking deep breaths. He looked up at the sky-reaching top of the pinnacle and had second thoughts. "Yeah," he said, "maybe next time."

Reiko laughed.

Before heading for Obaa-chan's home a few miles away, Reiko drove down the pinnacle and went down to the Ernie Pyle Memorial Park close by.

"It's a beautiful park," Chris said, studying the plants, flowers and the tall green trees surrounding the park. "Very quiet, very peaceful.

"Somebody must be taking good care of this place," he went on, looking at the white gate and fence around the park. And now reading the polished plaque about Ernie Pyle.

"Ojii-chan started it many years ago," she said. "Now, it's the island people who look after it."

"They know who Ernie Pyle was?"

"Ojii-chan made sure they all knew," she said.

"Your grandfather must've really looked up to Ernie Pyle," he said.

She nodded, and said nothing more. He'd know about it when the translation was finished.

From there, they went over to Obaa-chan's small, tile-roofed home. She had phoned Obaa-chan from home and Obaa-chan was waiting.

As always Obaa-chan not only greeted her with low bows, but with opens arms.

"Rei-chan…" And Obaa-chan covered her mouth with her hands, fighting back happy tears.

"Obaa-chan…"

It was always so wonderful to be in Obaa-chan's arms. Memories of her childhood visits to the island would come flooding back, and she would think nostalgically of those happy days she had spent with Obaa-chan and Ojii-chan.

"Oh, gomen nasai," Reiko apologized and introduced Chris.

Chris extended his hand, then quickly pulled it back and bowed respectfully.

"Ah, so," said Obaa-chan, "he is a professor at Ryudai."

"And also my English sensei," Reiko added.

"Just your English sensei?" Obaa-chan teased.

"Aw, Obaa-chan…"

Having brought the already translated Japanese version of Ojii-chan's Chronicle, Reiko handed it to Obaa-chan.

"There's more coming, Obaa-chan," she said. "I'll bring them when I'm finished translating them."

Obaa-chan held the Chronicle delicately, then caressed them. "Ojii-chan, I'm sure, is very happy that you are working so hard on the translation."

"I'm happy to be doing it, Obaa-chan."

Obaa-chan turned to Chris, and said in Nihongo, "Yamashiro-san, are you finding this interesting?"

Chris turned to Reiko.

"He'll read them when I'm through translating," she said to Obaa-chan.

"I hope you will find them interesting, Sensei." Understanding at least that much Japanese, Chris nodded, and said "Hai. I'm sure I will find them interesting."

Obaa-chan invited them into her home. Reiko, however, apologized and said she wanted to take Chris around the island before heading back to Naha.

Obaa-chan again hugged Reiko.

Reiko held Obaa-chan for a long moment, her mind racing back to Ojii-chan's Chronicle, hoping Obaa-chan will understand why Ojii-chan was so dedicated to the Ernie Pyle memorial park.

In about twenty minutes, they were at Reiko's secret beach spot.

Chris, not expecting a sandy secluded place on the tiny isle, ran down to the sandy shore. "C'mon," he invited, "it's like North Shore back home."

When Chris could not see her, Reiko quickly changed into her swimming outfit and ran through the tiny shoreline waves.

Before long, they were both splashing water at each other, then swimming out into the deep water where Chris was able to show what a great swimmer he was.

Back on shore, Reiko brought out the sandwiches and water she had brought in her picnic basket. They found shelter from the sunlight by moving under the shadows of the big boulders and laid their towels on the sand.

Chris was so relaxed and happy, she thought. He seemed to have completely forgotten about his classes, his family in Hawaii and even the threatening rainstorm.

"See," said Reiko, "isn't this a great spot?"

"Yeah," said Chris, "a great place. No one else comes here?"

"Not that I know of."

Now lying on their stomachs, each to each's own thoughts, Reiko was glad to be sharing her secret spot with Chris.

Chris was now looking out at the open sea before them, preoccupied.

"What's the matter, Chris?" she said, studying him.

He said nothing for a long moment, his eyes steadily up front.

"This spot reminds you of back home?"

Another moment of silence.

Then, "No," he finally said, "no, not back home. What happened yesterday."

"Yesterday?"

"He called me into his office," he began. "Takashi."

"Professor Miyazato?"

He nodded.

"Aren't you always seeing him in his office? Or, your office?"

"Not like yesterday."

She waited for him to go on.

"It's about you and me," he finally said.

And told her everything what he and Professor

Miyazato had talked about.

"It came all the way from the Chairman himself?" she asked.

He nodded.

"I...can't believe it," she said. "The Chairman of the department suspecting that..."

"Gossips are always exaggerated," he said. "By the time it gets up there, you can't tell how it got started."

Another round of silence.

"We can't be seen together anymore?" she finally said.

"According to Takashi the Chairman thinks very highly of you," he said.

"Then why is he questioning my judgement?"

"He just don't want you to jeopardize your standing with the university."

"Jeopardize? What's so wrong about being just friends with you?"

He shrugged.

"You think they're right?" she tested.

He shrugged again. "It not for me to decide."

"Then, you think it's best I keep away from you?"

"Reiko..." he said, "you're still very young. You have a whole life ahead of you. A great future with the university. Why...?" He shrugged again.

"I'm beginning to hate the university!" Reiko said. "How dare they tell me how I should live my life!"

"I want you to go on with your college life like everyone else," he said. "You and me, we'll be professor and student. As it should be."

Reiko fought back tears.

"Hey, c'mon," he said. "If I led you to believe anything good can come out of... Y'know... It's best we... We face it now before it's too late."

Finally. "What does Professor Miyazato think?"

"Takashi? We're good friends. For many years. As far as he's concerned, he's happy for us. –Even though he still doesn't know about Rose and me."

"What if the Chairman knew that you're about to get a divorce?" she questioned.

"Reiko," he said, "it's not just that I'm still a married man. It's you. Your life. I'm... I'm double your age. A daughter a year older than you. What's there for you?"

"Isn't that for me to decide?"

"Not when you don't know what you're getting into."

"I'm twenty-two. An adult. Besides, you're not going to be double my age forever.

He looked at her.

"When I'm twenty-three, you're not going to be forty-six."

He couldn't help from chuckling over that.

"You still haven't told me," she went on. "We're not going to keep seeing each other? Off or on campus?"

"In the classroom, yes."

"Chris! Are we going to or aren't we going to?"

"Reiko..." he said, again evasively.

"If we're not going to," she said, "I'll have to stop coming to your class."

"Oh, Christ..."

"Like you I'm a person of extremes. All black or all white."

"Y'know, you're not making it easy for me."
"Not making it easy for you?"
Another moment of silence.
Then, "...That big rainstorm," he said, "when did you say it's coming?"
"Chris!"
"I feel it's already hit us."

Chapter 18: Partial Moonlight

The rainstorm hit them. About three hours later.

They left the secret spot right after their anguishing talk and headed back to the harbor, Reiko remaining silent. Chris had difficulty making light of what they had talked about and now had no choice but to keep staring silently up front through the windshield.

The skies were still clear and the sun not yet dark from the threatening storm heading their way from the south.

They had missed the ferry and would have to wait an hour for the next ferry to arrive from Motobu.

"Hey," said Chris, looking up toward the pinnacle, "why don't we climb to the top. We have an hour to kill."

"You really want to?" she said, challenging.

"Sure," he said, glad she was still speaking to him.

They were at the base of the pinnacle in a few minutes, the parking lot now empty, the shops closed, their windows and doors boarded up.

Chris looked straight up at the top of the arrow-like pinnacle, and began to have second thoughts.

"C'mon," he finally said, "let's do it," and went over to the first steps, Reiko following.

"There's over 300 steps straight up to the top," Reiko warned. "You have to pace yourself or you won't make it."

"Hah," he dismissed, "I once climbed up Nuuanu Pali

higher than this."

"Yes, once. Many years ago," she said.

The climb was much tougher than he had envisioned. It was a steep, almost a straight-up climb, the narrow, unsteady concrete steps bordered by iron chains to hang on to. After the first one hundred steps, he had to pause to catch his breath. Then, again, after the next one hundred steps. When they finally reached the top, his legs were weary and unsteady. He was taking in long, hard breaths, his heart, though toughened from years of swimming, was pounding in his chest and throat.

Standing there at the rock-strewn, confining top, he gradually angled his way over to the edge, Reiko beside him. Slightly nervous looking down the steep ledge, he was suddenly rejuvenated. The 360 degree view down below and across the bay was spectacular. Breathtaking. Motobu and Nago were picture postcards, the white waves along their shoreline still an unceasing ebbing and flowing of a peaceful ocean scene.

Looking southward toward central Okinawa he could see the long endless shoreline almost down to Naha. Then, farther south, he could see dark rain clouds working their way up north.

"That's the rainstorm coming this way?" he asked.

"It's just the beginning," she said. "They'd get darker when the rains really start pouring and the winds get angrier."

Stepping gingerly to the eastern ledge, they could see the homes down below preparing for the rainstorm, the windows shut tight, the porches cleared, and the doors secured.

"Remember the Ie Jima drama I told you about?" Reiko said.

"About that girl?"

Reiko nodded. "Hando-gwaa. Down there is a small family museum with a statute of her. See it?"

Looking down beyond the jagged rocks, he could make out the life-size statute. "That girl," he said, "she really jumped down from up here?"

Reiko nodded. "It's a beautiful love story."

"If it had not actually happened."

"Then it wouldn't have been beautiful."

"You Okinawans," he said, "you take after the Naichis from the Mainland. Suicide is honorable and beautiful."

"If for a good reason."

"Is taking your own life ever a good reason?"

Reiko nodded.

Chris looked at her. She really meant it!

"Things always have a way of working out," he said, for lack of anything better to say.

She shut her eyes and pressed her hands together under chin in silent prayer.

"That girl," he said, "she didn't have to do it. She could've let time heal her pain."

Reiko's hands parted, her eyes focused steadily down below toward the museum.

"Not if the pain becomes unbearable," she said, her voice cracking, her eyes filled.

He fought himself. Then gave in.

He put his arms around her and held her.

She now held on to him, her warm wet cheek pressing against him.

They stood there a long moment, holding each other, comforting each other, sharing their plight together.

Chris kept thinking how in the world did he ever get into this? He knew he was vulnerable, going through what he was going through with Rose, but this kid, she's just a kid. He'd ruin her life. Take away her chance of meeting a nice college student her age.

All that was now academic. Because he cared for her. Very much. He missed her when she wasn't around. He missed her beautiful smile, her sweet girlish voice, her tender innocent way of speaking to him.

"Chris," she now said, dropping her arms from around him, "we better get going."

"Yeah," he said, "we better," and reluctantly dropped his arms.

While walking down the over-three-hundred steps, they could see that the winds had carried the dark clouds closer toward them, the waves along the shorelines no longer white, the brown brackish water washing in and out the debris to and from shore.

Their car was the only one returning to Motobu, a handful of passengers aboard all concerned about the threatening storm.

Driving off the ferry, Reiko quickly headed for the highway that led to the expressway. Chris, besides her, kept studying the dark clouds getting more ominous, the winds more threatening.

"You're sure it's safe to be driving right into the storm?"

he said.

"We still have a little time left before it really gets ugly," she said.

Midway down to Naha the relentless winds started rocking the car, the windshield wiper struggling to keep the window clear, the tires splashing heavy water under the fenders and against the doors.

They drove on into the sheets of rains that was not really a full rainstorm yet, the front lights of the car barely changing darkness into rays of lights. At the checkpoint, Chris paid the expressway attendant in a heavy raincoat from his side, and they continued on.

In a few more minutes, the statics in the car radio now screeching louder, the flashing lightning and roaring thunder more ominous, they kept listening to the announcer who was instructing drivers to keep away from certain streets in Naha where fallen trees had cut off the traffic.

"Oh, not that street to Nishihara!" Reiko mourned, swerving around slower cars, driving a little faster than she should be. "I won't be able to drive home."

"Can we make it to the apartment?" Chris asked.

"So far so good."

"You can spend the night in the extra bedroom," he said.

She gave him a sidelong glance.

They passed several cars involved in fender-benders, and finally arrived at Asato monorail station next to the apartment.

The wind, lightning and thunder were ferocious now.

Chris breathed a sigh of relief when Reiko finally drove down the side street into the apartment's parking lot. The open spot where she had parked earlier this morning was still empty.

They gathered whatever they could, jumped out of the car and rushed over into the ground level lobby drenched from head to foot.

Stepping out of the elevator on the third floor, leaving a trail of water on the walkway, they were at last in Chris' apartment.

He quickly offered Reiko a fresh towel from the shelf in the wash room, then reached for another for himself. He began wiping his wet dripping head and watched Reiko doing the same.

Somewhat drier, he changed into a pair of new beach shorts and T-shirt, then offered Reiko his one and only bathrobe. Which she took into the bathroom.

"Are you okay?" he asked.

He could hear her laughing.

"What's the matter?"

"You promise you won't laugh when I come out?"

In a few seconds, she stepped out of the bathroom, wiping her hair vigorously, the bathrobe hanging over her shoulders down to her feet.

"Hey," he said, "you look good in it," then couldn't keep from laughing.

"Oh, Chris."

"You better call home," he suggested, indicating the phone on the dining table. "They must be worried you're not home yet." She reached for the phone and dialed.

"Hello, Dad...

"Yes, I'm fine. We just got in...

"That's what we heard over the radio...

"I'm staying here at Professor Yamashiro's until it dies down or until I hear that the streets to Nishihara are cleared.

"No. He said he doesn't mind. If I have to stay overnight, he has an extra bedroom...

"Okay, Dad... Hai, oyasumi nasai... *Good night.*"

And she hung up, still wiping her hair.

Outside, the lightning continued streaking bright orange-red through the windows, followed by angry bursts of thunder crashing through the skies.

"Want some coffee?" he asked, stepping into the kitchen.

"Sounds great."

He came out of the kitchen with two cups of hot coffee, which he had heated in the microwave. He went back for cream and sugar.

"Was he worried, your dad?" he asked sitting across the dining room table from her.

"He was glad we didn't get stuck up in Motobu or Nago."

"What...about you might have to spend the night here?"

"He didn't approve. Nor did he disapprove."

"Trusts your judgment, huh?"

"Why wouldn't he? I was away from home while at UH, remember?"

"Yeah. Forgot your UH days."

They sipped their hot scalding coffee, glancing at each other over their coffee cups.

"What a day," she now said, rising, finishing her coffee. "The long ride, the long talks, finally ending with your first rainstorm."

"I was afraid I wouldn't experience any," he said.

"In Okinawa?" she said. "Just be prepared to go through the really bad ones. Plus a typhoon or two."

"You get used to them?"

"Typhoons? Nobody gets used to them."

'Your driving was great," he said. "A real pro."

"If you didn't notice how scared I am of lightning and thunder I guess I did okay."

Outside, the lightning and thunder were merciless.

"Chris," she said, "I'm glad we got to talk about…us."

He nodded.

"I'm getting into this with wide open eyes."

"You're sure?"

"Aren't you?"

He said nothing. He sipped more coffee, looking away.

"Well," she said, "my hair's a little drier. But my bathrobe is still a little too big."

"Just a little?" he teased.

Laughing, she turned and went into the extra bedroom.

"Chris?" she called. "If the streets are cleared, I'm driving home. Okay?"

"Be sure the streets are really cleared."

"I'll listen to the radio."

Now finished with his coffee, he was taking the cups into the kitchen when she called again.

"Chris."

"Yeah?"

"Have we really decided about us? You know…?"

"Have we?"

"I have. Haven't you?"

He did not reply.

"Of course," she went on, "I don't want you to be called into Chairman Asato's office."

"We'll see."

"Well… Good night…"

"Oyasumi nasai," he said, imitating her.

The lightning and thunder refused to let up.

He turned off the kitchen lights, went into his bedroom which was enclosed by paneled sliding doors, and settled to read in bed. It was the book he received from Amazon.Com. the other day, "Ernie Pyle's War" by James Tobin.

He'd read it, then pass it on to Reiko. It might help her with her translation.

His mind not quite into the book, he kept thinking of what happened earlier today. Especially at Reiko's secret spot, then up at the pinnacle where for the first time he had succumbed to his urge and held her in his arms.

He shouldn't have done it, he chided himself. It'd only lead to more urges.

Christ, his divorce isn't final yet. For all he knew, Rose might not even give him one. Just to spite him.

He'd always managed to stay away from attractive students before. Hands off! Lay off!

What got into him this time? She's just another student.

Well, not exactly. She's more mature than most of them. And more attractive. Still…

Boy! are you asking for it.

Is she really serious about suicide if the "Pain becomes unbearable?"

Naw. It's just a figure of speech. From a girl dramatizing a tragic scene.

She did say the girl "Hando-gwaa," in the drama actually did exist and did jump down the pinnacle.

Okinawans, he guessed, like the Japanese in Mainland Japan, loved tragedies. They loved and respected Yukio Mishima, the famous writer. Most approved his hara kiri suicide to show he was a true samurai dedicated to the Emperor. Others thought it was an overly dramatic, foolish gesture.

He went back to the Ernie Pyle book.

The events of the day kept coming back.

Howdahell did he let himself get this far with Reiko? he thought. She's just a kid taken in by what she thinks she really wants.

That's how it always gets started, he warned himself. A friendly, harmless interlude. Then… An old story.

God, she's pretty, he thought. And her innocence so attractive. From the very beginning. The plane ride from Honolulu and the long conversation sitting next to each other, then the sessions in his office, and the car rides all over Okinawa. He should've caught himself. Backed away. Like he always did in the past.

He wondered how she's doing with her translation? From what she's told him, it's a great Chronicle, about her grandfather's memories of the war. A Japanese ex-soldier revealing what perhaps is a greatest revelation in the Okinawan battles. Who killed Ernie Pyle? A machine gunner? A sniper? An unintended stray shot? It's been a mystery since day one when Ernie Pyle was shot on a remote unheard of tiny island off the coast of Okinawa.

"Chris!"

He jumped out of bed, slid the paneled door open, and stood there staring at her in her dragging bathrobe.

"I can't sleep," she said.

"The lightning and thunder?"

"And a strange bedroom."

He reached over and, holding her hands, brought her closer to him. Reaching down, he lifted her in his arms, backed into the chair and had her sitting on his lap, her arms around him.

"I'm usually not this frightened of rainstorms," she said. "It's the shadows of the lightning on the walls."

"I should have known better," he said. "Leaving you alone in a strange bedroom."

"I'll be all right when the lightning stop."

"Seems they'll never stop."

"They will. Suddenly. Like how they started."

Her lips were rubbing against his cheek as she spoke.

Instinctively, his own lips found hers, and he was now kissing her, her lips so soft, so warm, so tender…

Whattahell you doing!

He pushed her away, his head caught in a riptide.

"What's wrong?" he could hear her, still holding on to him.

It would be the most natural and expected thing for him to do, he said to himself. Carrying her into his bedroom.

Knock it off! For Chrissake! You're already in a "No-win" situation. You go through with it, you're...! Back off!

She was looking at him, puzzled, her eyes wide and unblinking.

What if you're the first man in her life? he told himself. If you're not the first man, what would you consider her? A college slut?

"Chris...?"

"Reiko. I'm not free. I'm not sure I'll ever be."

Jesus Christ! Whydahell was he making it so tough on himself. Go through with it. To hell with what happens.

"Hold me, Chris. Hold me."

Was moral teachings of youthful church-going days still governing him? Even after Rose?

And Carrie. How could he hope she'd never ever get involved in a situation like this. When he himself was caught up in one.

"Reiko..."

"Yes..."

"It's because I care for you very much that I'm...that we better not."

"You don't want to?"

"Yes. Very much. But..."

"You want to wait?"

"We better."

"Until things work out?"

He nodded.

Another long silence. "You've noticed?" she finally said.

"What?"

"The lightning and thunder, they're gone."

He listened. Carefully.

"Yeah," he said. "Yeah. They've stopped."

"And look," she said, turning toward the living room window, "the moon is out."

He looked out the window. "Yeah," he said, amazed. "Yeah, the moon is out. Just half. But nice and beautiful."

"And the stars…"

"Your yuta. On Kudaka island. What'd you think she's thinking watching the moon."

"It's a good omen," she said. "That's what she's thinking."

"Even though it's just a half-moon?"

"It's the beginning of a full moon."

Chapter 19:
The Spot

Anxious to show Chris her translations, Reiko was up late in her bedroom the following night rereading the last chapter. She had less than thirty pages to go. She'd split the thirty pages, leaving the second half, the most difficult, for the last chapter.

She wrote a few sentences, then a few paragraphs, and laid the pen down, her mind racing back to last night with Chris.

They did not discuss or mention their future. They knew, however, they'd have to avoid seeing each other on campus or near the campus. If he's ever called into the Chairman's office, it would mean that the Chairman would have to report him to the Dean of the Department, who, in turn, would have to report him to the President of the University. Chris would then have no choice but to resign and move back to Hawaii. With a bleak exchange professor's record.

Last night, she had expected Chris to carry her into his bedroom. When he did not she was hurt and disappointed that he did not desire her. Then glad he was willing to wait until he was free.

For a moment, she was reminded of wonderful Jimmy back in Honolulu who wanted to remain just a dear friend. But Chris wasn't like Jimmy. He had kissed her passionately and she could feel him fighting himself from going further.

Things will work out, she told herself. Yes, they will. There's no reason why she and Chris could not see each other openly on campus or any place else when Rose gives him a divorce.

Oh, Reiko! You better get back to the translation. "What will happen will happen," as Ojii-chan used to say. "Wishing for it to happen will not make it happen any sooner."

"You're so right, Ojii-chan" she said prayerfully. "Forgive me for having so many doubts about my life when you had to go through so much more than I would ever have to gaman *endure*."

She picked up her pen and, pushing aside all longings for last night, began writing.

The invasion of Okinawa by the Americans was on the first of April and it was now the middle of June and the fighting was still going on. How much longer will it go on? How many more Japanese and American soldiers, and Okinawan civilians would have to die before the battles stop?

We had seen the mighty Americans forces conquer Ie Jima in a matter of days. Our trucks, tanks, guns and artilleries were useless against the much more modern and powerful American armaments. Our machine guns were quite good, but they were slow and ineffective against the machine guns of the Americans. While our guns roared a hundred bullets at the Americans, their's spat out thousands at us.

Why can't Ushijima Taisho see the senselessness of continuing the fighting? Why can't the Emperor realize that the war is lost? Why must thousands of Nipponjin soldiers be slaughtered when they could be saved?

The Americans, as we knew now, were not the barbarians we have been told they were. Like us, they want the war to end so they could all return home. Like us, they have fathers, mothers, brothers and sisters and loved ones waiting for them.

I, of course, could not share my thoughts and feelings with my fellow POWs. Most of them were still fanatics. They still felt if one of us killed at least one American, the Americans would weaken and would stop their aggression.

It was unfortunate that my fellow POWs could not speak or understand a word of English and were not able to get to know an American soldier like my friend, Franky. Again, I hoped and prayed that Franky was all right, and would be able to return home safely to his family and to his future wife.

I don't know the exact day in June that news spread among us that Ushijima Taisho had committed hara kiri suicide in Mabuni. There were still pockets of battle raging in the South, but most of the Japanese soldiers had been killed or had blown themselves up with hand grenades or had been wounded and had been taken prisoners.

The battle of Okinawa was over, but not the war. We had heard that American troops were training to invade Mainland Japan, most likely Kyushu. For us POWs the war was over. There were countless of us in the Ishikawa camp. We had heard that some of the POWs were sent as far away as Hawaii.

They did not release us right away. We were still behind barbed wire fences waiting to go home. For us who were severely wounded or incapacitated, they started letting us out. Some of us had only one arm, some like me, just one leg, some who had suffered head injuries could barely speak, and there were those with only one eye or no eyes at all.

For me, I was fortunate to be able to function quite well by now. During the discharge procedure, I was told by the Nisei interpreter, Nakama-san, "The war is over for you, Oshiro-san. Go home. Start a new life."

"Hai," I said, bowing respectfully.

Nakama-san dug into his shirt pocket and brought out a fresh pack of cigarettes. "Here," he said, offering it to me. "I hope you'll have a peaceful life from here on."

Again, I bowed respectfully, grateful tears flooding my eyes. "Domo arigato gozaimashita." Thank you very much. Obaa-chan, not yet my wife, did not know of my release. The American army truck took several of us as far as Motobu and gave us our freedom. I was the only wounded POW from Ie Jima. There were no ferries, and I had to look for a fishing boat to take me home across the bay.

I had thought I would never see Gusuku Yama again. Now, approaching my island, my throat choking, I realized for the first time how beautiful and peaceful the mountain looked from a distance. It was even more beautiful and peaceful as the boat neared the shore.

It was still mid-morning, about the same time I was carried off the island on a stretcher that day by the Americans. I was now returning home, not completely whole, but at peace with myself and the world around me.

No one was there to greet me. I was a forgotten soldier returning home from the battlefields, struggling with the aid of crutches to keep me afloat, a wounded soldier who wished to be left alone the rest of his life and to be able to live a calm, peaceful life.

Rather than going directly home, I hobbled to the base of Gusuku Yama and looked up at the top. I was grateful that I had been spared to enjoy the luxury of the mountain's companionship. All my life I had lived on Ie Jima and had not known or appreciated the true beauty of the mountain. It was a monumental guiding light for all of us on the island; it was a kami-sama protecting us from evil spirits; and it was a spiritual haven for our ancestors who had gone on ahead of us.

I kept ambling along until coming to a small stretch of open land with a rough wooden plaque at the front. This must be the place I had heard about. Where the great American newspaper reporter was buried.

There was no fence around the grave site at that time. Just a few bouquet of flowers around a fresh mound of dirt below me.. I stepped up to the plaque. It said: "AT THIS SPOT, THE 77ᵀᴴ INFANTRY DIVISION LOST A BUDDY, ERNIE PYLE, 18 APRIL 1945."

The flowers were placed there by GIs who were still mourning over the death of their beloved friend, I told myself.

Suddenly curious by the plaque's beginning words, "AT THIS SPOT..." I looked around the flat edges of the mountain, then at its top and the surroundings. Whoever shot Ernie-san must have had a clear view of him, I concluded. I looked around again at the different viewpoints and my eyes drifted, then quickly shifted to the pillbox my companions and I had occupied.

Not wanting to even think that the shot could have come from our pillbox, I again looked at the other viewpoints. The only other pillbox nearby had been to our right occupied by Sergeant Morikawa and his men.

Now, recalling the last few moments of my semi-

consciousness, I could not help but believe that it was possible Ernie-san had been shot from the direction of our pillbox. Hesitantly, reluctantly, I hobbled toward the partly-destroyed pillbox about 150 kilos away. It was partly entangled by young vines, wild grass and low branches.

Struggling, I crawled down into the narrow, dirt-covered pillbox and looked out at the "SPOT" through a small window opening."

"No!"

I looked at the "SPOT" again.

"No!"

Reiko stopped. She laid the pen down. Knowing from the Japanese version what followed, she needed a break.

She took a deep breath before going on.

Chapter 20:
The Pronouncement

In the classroom the following Monday, Chris' eyes swung back to Reiko in her usual front seat, and they exchanged warm private smiles before he directed his attention back to the class.

As the class discussed "From Here To Eternity," Chris had difficulty focusing on the assignments. His eyes would return to Reiko, and his mind would flash back to the dreamlike day they had spent together on Ie Jima and the evening they had been together at his apartment before she went home.

There was no backing away now. No more decisions to be made. No more doubts, no more guilt, no more ways to get out of the situation. And it made him feel like a young college kid.

Only now, unlike those young college days, the future was not as bright nor as promising as he'd wish they were.

Douglas had not yet sent him the divorce papers to sign. And there was no explanation. Has Rose changed her mind about the Kailua property? Is she being her bitchy self and making him sweat it out? Worse, she now doesn't want a divorce?

All that hardly mattered now.

He's found a new life. With Reiko. Someone he'll be together with from now on. If that makes him sound like a damn fool forty-four-year-old kid it sure is great to feel like a kid again.

Reiko was looking his way again. And she was smiling that warm, almost shy smile of hers. Oh, jeesus. How could an old fart like him feel his heart pumping up in his throat just looking at her?

When the bell rang and class was over, Reiko stepped up to him. "I'm almost finished with the translation," she said, confidentially.

"Hey, that's great," he said. "When can I read them?"

"In a week," she replied. "Maybe."

"Takashi is waiting for it, too."

"I still have to go through the hardest part," she said. "The ending."

"The hardest part about any writing is the ending," he said. "Because you don't want it to end.

"Just write it as simply as you can," he added.

"I saw the dog; the dog saw me?" she paraphrased what he had once told her.

"And you ain't gonna say it better than that."

"Hai, Sensei," she said. "I'll remember that."

"Your Ojii-chan," Chris went on, "he really went through a lot, huh?"

"I thought I knew him," she said.

"You didn't?"

She shook her head. "Now I know why he didn't want to talk about the war."

"Those who really went through it want to forget it," he said.

She nodded, agreeing.

"Poor Ojii-chan," she said. "Keeping everything to himself."

"He had you to reveal what he went through," he said.

"Yes. Finally."

"And now you can share them with us," he said.

"As soon as I can," she said.

After a moment, he said, "I guess you know, no more lunches at the cafeteria for us."

"This university!" she said bitterly.

"Just be a little patient," he said. "Things will work out."

"…I better be going to my next class," she said. I'll call you tonight. Okay?"

Nodding, he watched her stepping over to the door to put on her shoes, again feeling like a young kid. God, he loved her, he thought, exchanging warm smiles and waving boyishly.

When he got home and searched his e-mail, he wanted to smash his computer against the wall!

Douglas had finally written.

Rose refused to sign the divorce papers, it began. *She claims infidelity on your part. An affair you're having over there. She still wants one-half of the Kailua farmland as originally filed.*

Whattahell is she talking about, an affair you're having over there? If true she can make it nasty and rough.

That goddamn bitch! Chris pounded his fist into his hand. That..! She's bluffing. How can she know anything about him and Reiko? Unless… You can't put it pass her. She'd do it. Have somebody here in Okinawa spy on him.

You can deny it, said Douglas. *On the other hand, if there's any substance to what she claims… We might have to consider giving in if you want a quick divorce. Or keep dragging it on forever.*

Substance? What substance? He and Reiko are just friends. ...Well...

And he had thought everything was going great. Rose would sign the papers and avoid a court battle; not damage her reputation as an up-righteous, church-going community leader.

Maybe he should give in. Let her have half of the Kailua property. To hell with it. Win some; lose some.

Then, picturing Rose's smug expression, he could not give in. Just could not! That...! She's the one cheated on him! She's the one made a damn fool out of him!

He won't give in. Shit no! He'd fight her all the way. To the Supreme Court if he has to. She's willing to stake her reputation, he's willing also. Let the chips fall wherever...

He wrote *Douglas back:*

No way! If she wants a court battle and air out her dirty laundry, that's fine with me. My grandfather worked hard all his life for that property. His sacrifices are not going to be ditched because some bitch sees money signs attached to it.

Tell her no holds barred. Even if Carrie has to suffer because of her mother's goddamn affair.

CHRIS.

He went over to the refrigerator, took out a bottle of beer, and gulped a long pull. It felt good. Reckless. Invigorating.

You want to play hard ball, you no-good bitch, you're in for it!

Chapter 21: Revelations

She had promised Chris that she would have the translations finished in another week. She had not realized that the ending would be more difficult than she thought. She had to rearrange the paragraphs so that they would be in sequence.

After weeks and months of struggling and laboring through Ojii-chan's writings she was relieved but sad that she was coming to the end. She had gotten together with Ojii-chan as though he had come back to her. And now he would soon be saying sayonara again.

Where she had left off the other night was agonizing.

She read the last chapter once more.

She began where she had stopped.

No!

I looked at the SPOT again.

No!

Several tree branches were blocking my view, but it must have been clear two months ago.

Desperately, I tried to erase the scene, and succeeded for a moment. Then it came back.

We did as we were ordered by Sergeant Morikawa not to open fire until the enemy was almost upon us.

A breathless moment went by. We suddenly opened fire with both of our machine guns.

The enemy quickly recovered from the unexpected burst of our machine guns and pinpointed their guns, grenades and artilleries into Sergeant Morikawa's pillbox and ours . In a matter of seconds, we were shredded to pieces, my companions all dead. At that moment I believed I, too, was dead. But the excruciating pain in my right leg and my head assured me that I was still alive.

I crawled over to the displaced machine gun and quickly adjusted it to fire the last belt of bullets at the advancing enemy. For a long moment, everything around me took on a silence so deafening that I thought I was dead. I rubbed away blood flowing down my face into my eyes and shook my head to escape the numbness overcoming me.

I had been flying in and out of consciousness and had lost track of time.

Then I thought I heard a truck approaching from the beach. It was a jeep. With several soldiers. Summoning all the strength still remaining in me, I aimed the machine gun in their direction. I pressed the trigger. In the next moment, I blacked out.

I was now barely aware of what was going on. I had missed the jeep. The Americans had jumped out and were hiding in a ditch along the dirt road.

Bleary-eyed, rubbing the blood off my forehead and eyes, I could see movements ahead of me.

Again, shaking my head to clear the cobwebs, I could make out the vague figures. When I pressed the trigger I could hear a burst of a machine gun accompanying mine from Sergeant Morikawa's direction.

The Americans retaliated instantly from every direction imaginable and charged our pillbox.

I now truly believed I was dead.

But I could hear voices. American voices that I could somehow make out.

"Let me finish him off!" I could hear one of the Americans saying. "Let me finish him off!"

"He's our prisoner!" the other said.

"You know who this bastard just killed!"

"He's a POW!"

"We took care of the others! This bastard, he's the only one still alive!'

"I'm ordering you! Lay off him or you're up for court martial!"

The soldier's rifle, as well as the rifles of the others, moved away from my head, some of the soldiers swearing, some speaking in low mournful tones, others in weeping voices.

Until then I did not know if I had actually killed one of them or not. Now I knew. I had fulfilled my duty of killing one of them before they killed me.

The terrible pain in my right leg took on a merciful numbness, and in a few seconds I was not able to feel anything. I realized then that one of them had given me a morphine shot.

Another vague sequence followed. I was being carried on a stretcher. To where I had no idea. Or did not care. I had carried out my duty. I was prepared to die.

Now, looking out through the narrow opening at the "SPOT" I realized that the man I had shot was not a soldier.

It was Ernie Pyle!

I had killed Ernie-san! Someone who had no intention of killing me.

I was a murderer!

Why? Why did it have to be me! Why did it have to be me who killed him!

I thought of Franky. What would Franky think of me?

And what about all the common American soldiers? And all the American families who believed in Ernie-san. What would they think of me? Me, who was saved by the GIs, turns out to be the enemy who shot Ernie Pyle!

I could still remember that all of us had been issued hand grenades. The others had attached the grenades to their belt buckles while I had hidden mine under a concrete slab, hoping to attach it to my belt later.

I crawled over and searched for it.

It was still there.

I dug it out.

Shutting my eyes and resolved to commit my last act as a soldier, I dropped down to my knees. I placed the grenade down before me and, placing my hands together, prayed for forgiveness.

I picked up the grenade. I yanked the pin out. And stuck the grenade into my belly.

One, two, three, four, five...

Nothing happened.

I pounded the grenade into the concrete slab and stuck it deeper into my belly.

Six, seven, eight, nine, ten!

It would not explode!

The tension depleted whatever strength remaining in me. I collapsed and began to cry. Softly, then out loud.

Death had cheated me once before here in the pillbox. It was cheating me again.

And Reiko weeping, could not go on. The tragedy was

not that Ojii-chan might have shot Ernie Pyle; it was that he believed he did.

Ojii-chan. Oh, Ojii-chan.

Chapter 22: Missing Chapter

When Chris read the translations, he, too, was moved to tears.

Reiko had brought them to his apartment two days ago. Missing was the final chapter which she was still working on. She was struggling with it, she said.

Not having any classes the next day, he had spent all day and most of the evening reading the translations.

When Reiko came over last night, they went to dinner in faraway Oroku town. Reiko seemed a great burden was lifted off her shoulders. She had delivered the first half of the Japanese version to Obaa-chan and would soon be delivering the second half.

After dinner, they had driven back to the apartment where Chris had a bottle of beer, Reiko, her usual tea. They had refrained from discussing the translations. They'd wait until Reiko was finished with the last chapter.

Chris was relieved and excited over Reiko's translations. He had been afraid they'd be boring and uninteresting. As he kept reading, he was struck by Reiko's story-telling ability. She knew how to capture the reader's interest and sustain that interest throughout.

It was, of course, Ojii-chan's story. But it was Reiko's approach to the material that made it captivating and a page-turner. Although Ojii-chan had addressed the story personally to Reiko, it was actually aimed at a vast audience. It was mesmerizing. Almost as though it did not really happen. Yet, the truth was all there. It could not possibly have been Ojii-chan's imagination. He was not a novelist; he was a historian who sought to record the horrendous devastations not only to Okinawa, but to himself personally.

Chris' biggest concern had been Reiko's writings would follow a pattern of clichés, flowery words and trite phrases. Most college students were victims of it. Reiko, however, avoided that pattern. Maybe it's because Ojii-chan himself had avoided it.

Chris had always advised his students to write as simply as possible. Avoid looking up words in the dictionary. If you have to you are not using the right word. Good writing is innate, he had always maintained. If you don't feel the word deep down in your gut, it doesn't belong there. And Reiko had followed that rule.

Next day, Chris went to Takashi's office and handed him the manuscript. He dared him to stop reading it once he started.

"That good, eh?" said Takashi.

"It's great," Chris said. "A classic tragedy. Another Rashomon."

"Aw, c'mon."

"No kidding, Takashi. Like Akutagawa's Rashomon, you're left hanging. Who really did it?"

"Well," said Takashi, "I better get to it right away."

Chris did not warn Takashi about the missing last chapter.

When Chris finally told Reiko how much he had enjoyed her translations, she let out a great sigh of relief. She had been afraid of his criticisms, and had avoided him for a couple days, including the classroom.

Now that Professor Miyazato was reading the manuscript she went into another round of gut-wrenching anxiety.

"What if he thinks it's awful," she said at the apartment.

"He already said that," he said.

"What!"

Chris laughed.

"Chris! Did he really say that?"

Again laughing, Chris held her in his arms.

"Chris!"

He called me into his office this morning," he said.

"And?"

"Except for the ending he loves it!" Chris finally relented. "He agrees. It's a classical tragedy."

"Except for the missing ending," Reiko said, laughing.

'He plans to show it to the Chairman of the Department," he said.

"Professor Asato!"

"He thinks it's that good."

"Oh, Chris, what an honor for Ojii-chan! Having the Chairman of the English Department reading his Chronicle."

What Chris did not tell Reiko was what Professor Asato had told Takashi about Chris and Reiko seen together at a restaurant in American Town in Yomitan and also at the lobby of Harbor View Hotel.

"Chris," Takashi had said, "if the Chairman feels he has to pass that information on to the Dean of the Department it can be bad."

"No warning next time, eh?" Chris had said.

Takashi had shaken his head. "The Dean would have no choice. He'd have to pass it on to the President."

"And, I'd be on my way back to Hawaii?"

"Let's hope it won't come to that," Takashi had said, avoiding Chris' eyes.

Chapter 23:
To Last Shot

It took three attempts to start the next chapter.

The first attempt, she translated the first few pages, printed them, then crumpled them. The second attempt, she tried another angle. Instead of translating them, she rewrote Ojii-chan's Nihongo *Japanese* in a more cohesive and simpler manner, translated them, then printed them. She still was not satisfied.

It was on the third attempt that she decided to split the chapter. Do the first half now and the second half later. She began:

You've come this far, Rei-chan, and I'm grateful. I started writing this about a year ago just when you were leaving for the University in Hawaii.

You were always a good student in both Japanese and English schools. My wish when I began this was that you would submit it to our Japanese newspapers here in Okinawa or on the Mainland. My other wish was for you to find an American publisher who would be willing to publish your translations. I feel Americans should know what really happened to Ernie-san here on Ie Jima.

I should have written this long ago. I kept putting it off. Until I found books written about the battles of Okinawa. The books, in English, were well researched and well written. A couple of them were the latest biographies of Ernie Pyle, who was buried here until his remains were transferred to an American Military Cemetery in Hawaii.

You know now why I have dedicated my life to Ernie-san's Memorial Park. Yes, his remains are in Hawaii. His spirit, however, will always remain here with us. This is where he took his last final breath; this is where he had wished to write his last words about the horrors and senselessness of wars; and, this is where he was killed by a foolish and misled young Japanese soldier who had thought he was doing his duty.

The biographies of Ernie-san said that those who were with him that day recalled seeing him raising his head from the ditch to look around him. It was then he was suddenly killed by a single machine gun bullet to his head.

I remember aiming my machine gun toward the direction of the "SPOT," but I can't remember seeing any heads rising from the ditch. All I know is that I fired at blurred movements before me.

Sergeant Morikawa and his men, who were to the right of me, started firing their machine guns at the advancing Americans. That meant they were able to see the "SPOT" too.

Could it mean! No. It can't be. I had a better view of the Americans. They were much closer to me.

But a single shot to Ernie-san's head! Machine gun bullets would have spread all over him.

Could he have been shot by one of our snipers hiding near the SPOT?

That, of course, would have spared me. I was not responsible for Ernie-san's death!

Chapter 24: The Ring

Right after Reiko left last night, he had checked his e-mail. And was astounded. Overwhelmed. He had to read it a second time before it finally registered.

Douglas said: *Chris, this should make you believe in miracles. Carrie walked into my office a few minutes ago and handed me the divorce papers.*

I asked Carrie, trying not to sound too surprised, when did your mother sign these? This morning, she said. I acted as if I had expected the papers signed, sealed and delivered to my office any day.

How is your mother? I asked Carrie. I hoped Rose and I are still friends.

That's when Carrie told me she had known all along about her mother's affair with that guy at the bank. She warned her mother if the divorce went to court and all the "stink" came out, she was leaving home and would never return.

Need more be said?

Go ahead and enjoy your own affair.

DOUGLAS.

Chris wanted to call Reiko, then decided to wait and surprise her tomorrow. He had to drink an extra bottle of beer to calm himself, and be able to fall asleep.

Early next morning, Chris was in giant Mitsukoshi Department store on Kokusai Dori, an excited forty-four-year-old young boy. He went directly to the jewelry department and spoke to the elegantly dressed middle-aged saleslady. When Chris spoke to her in his Hawaiian-accented Japanese, the saleslady politely changed from Japanese to English. Which was quite good. Much better than his Japanese.

"You are lookin' for en-gage-ment ring?" she said, delightedly sharing his excitement.

"Hai," Chris responded, trying to be a stoic Japanese.

"You are visitor here?" asked the lady, attempting a conversation.

"Well, yes and no," he said. "I'm an exchange professor at Ryudai."

"Ah, so," she said, "a professor at Ryudai."

Chris nodded, looking at the jewelry in the showcase.

"Ring for galfriend?"

"Hai."

"You know size? Of finger?"

"I'll have to have her try it on. Okay?"

"If not fit just-a right," said the lady, "bring back. Try 'nother one."

The saleslady was now behind the showcase placing several engagement rings on the glass top. Hardly knowing anything about engagement rings, he studied one then another, remembering that when he and Rose got married he couldn't afford an engagement ring. Just a wedding band.

"Galfriend, big? Small? Skinny?"

"She's about your size," he said. But, he wanted to add, much younger.

"Oh, 'bout me?" said the lady. "Then t'is one, I t'ink is ring for galfriend?"

He looked at the diamond-studded ring, hoping it wouldn't cost an arm and a leg. Although he was much better financially now than when engaged to Rose, he was still his old conservative self. For a moment, just for a moment, he remembered asking Rose to marry him, and the moment brought back fond memories of her. She certainly wasn't a bitch then and maybe she won't be any more now that Carrie had straightened her out. Poor Rose, he thought. And the magnanimous moment quickly faded.

Later that morning, he called Reiko from his office and asked her to come over before class started.

"Chris, you're sure that's wise?" she said, concerned.

"Wiser than you think," he said.

"Professor Miyazato, he might see me up there."

"He'll approve."

"Of you and me together on campus?"

"Just get your okole up here."

"I'm already up there," she said.

In less than half-an-hour, Reiko was at his office door, breathing hard. She had rushed over to the faculty building from the faraway parking lot and had raced up the stairways to the third floor.

"Chris, is something wrong?" she said, alarmed.

"Shut the door," he commanded.

She did.

"Come here."

She looked at him, not moving.

"Come here."

She stepped forward slowly.

He took out the tiny, delicate box from his pants pocket, and handed it to her.

"Open it."

"Chris, what is it?"

"C'mon. Open it."

She untied the colorful ribbon, and opened the box.

"Chris!"

She kept looking at its content. "You're sure…!?"

"Hey, I'm the professor; you're the student."

Tears flooded her eyes. Not bothering to wipe them away, she rushed into his arms.

"Oh, Chris… And I was afraid you'd have to go back to Hawaii."

"Hey, no pau hana ovah heah yet," he said in pidgin. "Must-a keep teachin' heah even afta' we get married."

"You no bull-lie," she said, joining his pidgin. "You, for real, wanna marry me?"

"Hey, whuddya t'ink? I gonna fool 'round with somet'in' serious like marriage?"

"Oh, Chris! " She refused to let go of him.

His eyes misty, his throat tightening, he thought, for Chrissake, you're acting like a young kid on his first date.

They rushed over to Takashi's office down the hallway. Without preliminaries, they announced their engagement, and Reiko very excitedly extended her hand and showed him the ring.

Takashi seemed puzzled. Having met Rose during the Honolulu days and having been told by Chris that he and Rose were not getting along, Takashi apparently thought it was just a passing phase. Not a divorce!

No need to elaborate, Chris thought, exchanging eye contact with Takashi. He'll explain everything to him some other time.

Takashi, now recovered, smiled a quick smile, still a little puzzled. He bowed to Chris, then to Reiko. "Omedetto." *Congratulations.* "Now I don't have to hear anymore rumors about you two?" he said.

"Rumors?" Reiko said.

"And a warning from the Chairman of the Department," Takashi went on.

"Warning!" Reiko's hand jumped up to her mouth.

Chris reached over and held her hand. "It's gonna be okay."

"C'mon," said Takashi, "let's go over and see him."

Three of them walked across the campus to the chairman's office.

Takashi led them to the chairman's door, and knocked.

After a second knock, the door opened and Asato-sensei, the mid-fifties Chairman, stood there studying Chris, Reiko, then Takashi. In a dark suit, his thin dark hair combed neatly to the side, his stunned expression gradually faded into a faint smile.

"Miyazato-sensei, come in, please come in," he now said to Takashi in English. "You, too, Yamashiro-sensei and Kinzo-san."

The Chairman led them into his confined, undecorated office. "Here," he said, indicating the three chairs before his desk, "sit here," and went behind his desk.

"Nice to see you again, Yamashiro-sensei," he said

politely. Then to Reiko, "Kinjo-san, I finally finished your grandfather's Chronicle."

"Oh?" Reiko was startled. "Domo arigato gozaimasu for taking time from your busy schedule to read it," she managed to say.

"After what Miyazato-sensei told me about it, I couldn't wait to read it," said the Chairman, sitting. "It is remarkable. Not only a truly fine piece of writing, but an amazing account of what really happened there at Ie Jima during the war."

Reiko thanked the Chairman again.

"If it's all right with you," the Chairman added, "I'd like to send it to an English publisher friend in Tokyo."

"Oh, Sensei!" Reiko cried out, "That would be wonderful! "

"By the way," the Chairman went on, "there's no title."

"Ohmygod..." said Reiko, "gomen nasai. Excuse me, Sensei. I completely forgot that Ojii-chan did not have a title."

"The Chronicle is about your grandfather and Ernie Pyle," said the Chairman. "Why not call it, Ojii-chan and Ernie Pyle?"

"Why, yes. Of course," Reiko agreed. "Ojii-chan and Ernie Pyle."

She turned to Chris. "What do you think?"

"Makes you wonder what it's all about," Chris said.

"An honor for your grandfather to be on the title with Ernie Pyle," Takashi said.

Chris, taking everything in, and proud of Reiko, wondered how long this was going to go on.

"Well, Kinjo-san," the Chairman went on, "you're one step closer to finishing your graduate studies."

Again, Reiko thanked the Chairman.

A moment of silence.

"Ah, Asato-sensei," Takashi took over, "about those reports… Yamashiro-sensei and Kinjo-san seen together…"

"Ah, yes," said the Chairman, avoiding everyone's eyes, "it's disturbing. Very disturbing."

Chapter 25: Speeches

The transition in Ojii-chan's last two chapters did not seem right. She wrote and rewrote them, at last tying the chapters together.

Much better now, she went on:

When I first came to Ernie-san's grave and blamed myself for his death, I vowed to become the caretaker of his grave site. I planned to plant trees and flowers and build a fence around the open space. I would paint the fence a glowing white so that when visitors came to pay their respects to Ernie-san, they would remember Ernie-san's glowing life and his memorable writings.

Not long afterward, I received my high school diploma from Nakijin High School across the bay and started to teach at our local grade school. When Okinawa had its first university, I moved to Naha City and received my degree in education. I then became a high school teacher in the Motobu-Nago area. I began teaching English to our young students and always told them about the wonderful writings of Ernie-san.

Being a veteran who survived the war and always conspicuous because of my missing leg, I began receiving invitations to speak about the Ie Jima battle at various gatherings in our villages. Before long, I was invited to speak at high schools and universities. This gave me opportunities to speak about Ernie-san and his sacred memorial park.

Unexpectedly, people began to fictionalize my role as a

soldier. They claimed I was a samurai who battled the enemy with no fear of death. Then, at one of the gatherings, when someone asked how many Americans I had killed, I realized I had let my speeches turn me into war hero. I quickly changed my speeches and began speaking about the horrors of war.

Soon, I began receiving invitations to speak at Christian churches.

My only knowledge of Christianity was that it followed the teachings of Jesus Christ. When one of the followers tried to teach me Christianity, I told him that I believed in the Okinawan religion of ancestral worship.

Nevertheless, I started attending Christian services, especially at a Baptist Church in Okinawa City. I received a measure of comfort and inspiration from its teachings.

Throughout my invitations to speak about the war, I became aware that the older generations who survived them were still having nightmares. The younger generations, on the other hand, who heard about the destructions and killings from their parents, grandparents, uncles and aunts, the war was a historical past.

To some of the young people who seemed to glorify the brave Japanese soldiers who had perished in the battlefields, I spoke of the fears, sufferings and horrors of soldiers wounded and dying, and that wars are not adventurous nor glorious, but terrible wastes of precious human lives.

Chapter 26: The Engagement

The Chairman now spoke directly to Chris. "Our policy. About professors and students... I told Miyazato-sensei to explain to you. Possible conflicts. I guess he did not emphasize enough..."

"Yes, he did," Chris interfered.

"Then why are you violating our policy, Yamashiro-sensei."

"Ah, Asato-sensei," Takashi cut in. "We are here to explain he will no longer be violating our school policy."

"Our school policy is: a professor is not to be romantically involved with a student."

"Even with a student he is going to marry?" Takashi said.

Chairman Asato looked at Takashi; over at Chris and Reiko.

Reiko showed the Chairman her ring.

The Chairman stared at the ring. Silently.

Then cleared his throat. "Ah, so," he finally said.

Chris exchanged warm triumphant smiles with Reiko.

"You've gotten a divorce from your wife, Yamashiro-sensei?" the Chairman wanted to know.

"Hai," said Chris. "It'll be final any day."

"Well," said the Chairman, rising from his chair and coming over, "I don't see how you're violating our school policy when you plan to get married."

The Chairman reached for Chris' hand and shook it vigorously.

"Omedetto," the Chairman said. *Congratulations.*

He then stepped over to Reiko and, bowing deeply, said "Omedetto, Kinjo-san."

"Domo arigato gozaimasu," Reiko responded. *Thank you very much.*

Turning to Takashi, the Chairman said, "You knew about their engagement and never told me about it?"

"Ah, Sensei," said Chris, "Miyazato-sensei found out just a few minutes ago."

"So did I," said Reiko.

Puzzled, the Chairman studied three of them.

"It must be a Hawaiian custom," he finally said, "the girl the last person to know she's engaged."

"I didn't give her a chance to think it over," Chris said.

"Another Hawaiian custom?" the Chairman said, smiling vaguely at Chris and Reiko.

"I hope you'll be able to come to our wedding, Sensei," Reiko said.

"When will that be?"

"We haven't decided yet," said Chris. "I'm hoping it'll be right after I'm over my exchange program."

"You're going to need an extension if you want Kinjo-san to get her master's before you leave."

"Well, yes. I've been thinking about that, too," said Chris.

"So, Sensei," Reiko said eagerly, "will you come to our wedding?"

"After what you two have been putting me through, you expect me not to?" said the Chairman, chiding Reiko. "Nothing is going to keep me away. Not even wild horses, to coin that American phrase."

Laughing, Reiko bowed gratefully.

Chapter 27: Sayonara

She had shared Ojii-chan's agony and pain throughout the Chronicle. At last the ending!

She took a deep breath, and began:

It is puzzling that world leaders who start wars are always claiming that Kami-sama God is on their side. Doesn't the other side have a Kami-sama, too?

Ancestral Worship, our belief, seems something out of ancient times when what it really is worshiping those who had gone ahead of us. Just before leaving us they had all enjoyed peaceful and tranquil last moments. Why can't we learn to live those last moments in our daily lives?

Our island and the rest of Okinawa had lived quiet, peaceful lives until the invasion by the Mainland Japanese. The Naichis, as we called them, abolished our kingdom and government, and replaced them with their own system of emperor and dictatorship.

But they could not replace our spiritual belief. Our belief was beyond their teaching of Buddhism.

Then came the American conquerors. They made us believe in their worldly ways, but could not change our spiritual ways.

I have been very fortunate to have lived here on Ie Jima most of my life, Rei-chan. Our island is like that isolated mountain village in faraway China where all is well and people live forever. We do not live forever. But we live longer than the rest of the world, because we are happy people.

According to the teachings of our ancestors, nothing is ever permanent. The trees, the mountains and the sands are forever changing. We accept those changes and change our lives accordingly.

When we waved sayonara to each other that day you were leaving for Hawaii, Rei-chan, I knew we would never see each other again.

I was told by my doctor that I had terminal stomach cancer and I had less than a year to live. I did not want to have an operation. It would take months to get over the operation and I would not be able to finish this.

I have enjoyed a very good life, Rei-chan. I not only survived the war, I was given a chance to learn that the goodness of man far outweighs his hatreds, his bitterness and his anger.

I have always tried to give back more than was given me, and I believe I succeeded in some ways. My only regret, which I had to live with throughout my life, was that I was responsible for the death of a great man who was loved, respected and honored by everyone.

Whenever you are at the Memorial Park, Rei-chan, please offer an osenko to Ernie-san for me.

I will soon be joining him.

Sayonara, Rei-chan.

Ojii-chan.

Reiko choked back a burst of sobs.

The long journey was finally over. She had relived her life with Ojii-chan all these months and had become closer to him than ever before. She must now go on with her own life.

She suddenly remembered Dr. Sweeney. She must not put off another day writing him. She turned the computer to a blank page and began:

Dear Dr. Sweeney:
Enclosed is a translated copy of my grandfather's Chronicle. I'm sorry I took this long to send it to you. The Japanese version of the Chronicle was quite long and I had difficulty translating parts of it.

I was tempted to write to you before I finished the translation. I'm glad I did not. I could never have been able to replace Ojii-chan's warm memories of you with my own words, nor could I have been able to express his deep appreciation for what you did for him during his painful, despairing days.

When I met you and Mrs. Sweeney I had not yet read the Chronicle and so I did know the full extent of your friendship with Ojii-chan. As you will note, he was forever grateful to you for giving him faith, hope and belief.

He had never mentioned to anyone, not even to Obaa-chan grandmother, why he had dedicated his life to the Ernie Pyle Memorial Park. I feel he wanted to tell me about it, but could not.

He was tortured by the awful tragedy all of his life. Finally, when he allowed himself to write about it, he must have felt forgiven. Not entirely; but partially and mercifully.

Thank you, Dr. Sweeney, for having been so very kind to Ojii-chan. Out of his terrible experience in the war, he learned from you that men might hate collectively, but very seldom personally. It is a lesson I, too, will always remember

Sayonara,
Reiko Kinjo.

Title: Lucky Come Hawaii

- • Author: Jon Shirota
- Publisher: Univ of Hawaii Pr; 1 edition
- Paper Back: ISBN: 9780824834487
- Number of pages: 188
- Publication Date: January 2010

In the opening chapter of this classic novel set in Hawai'i, news of the attack on Pearl Harbor has just reached rural Maui. Miscommunication, confusion, and rumors of war aggravate the already tense relations among the diverse immigrant communities, Native Hawaiians, and the American military.

As told through the perspective of a poor Okinawan family, *Lucky Come Hawaii* vividly captures the emotions and trauma at this momentous turning point in Island history, which will change the fate of individuals, ways of life, and the land itself forever. First published in 1965 to national acclaim is now back in print.

Lucky Come Hawaii is a tale of love, intrigue, humor, and Island families torn apart and reunited by the events of December 7th. The novel also anticipates the changes overtaking Hawaii, from Territory to Statehood, from small towns to a militarized Pacific metropolis. *Lucky Come Hawaii* should be required reading for anyone who cares deeply about the untold stories of the Islands' multi-ethnic communities and the struggle of individuals to find a place and sense of identity in their American home.

www.ingramcontent.com/pod-product-compliance
Lightning Source LLC
Chambersburg PA
CBHW022215090526
44584CB00012BB/560